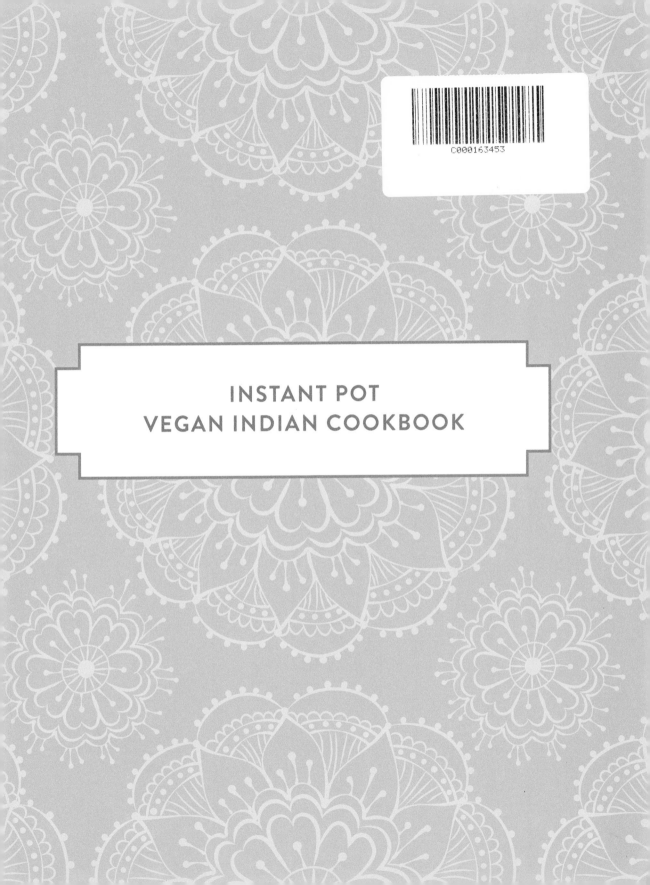

INSTANT POT
VEGAN INDIAN COOKBOOK

INSTANT POT

VEGAN INDIAN

COOKBOOK

· · · · · · · · · · · · · · · ·

80 QUICK AND EASY PLANT-BASED FAVORITES

MEENA AGARWAL

PHOTOGRAPHY BY
ANDREW PURCELL

ROCKRIDGE
PRESS

Cover Designer: Eric Pratt
Interior Designer: Julie Schrader
Art Producer: Samantha Ulban
Editor: Anna Pulley
Production Editor: Rachel Taenzler
Production Manager: Riley Hoffman

Photography © 2021 Andrew Purcell. Food Styling by Carrie Purcell.

ISBN: Print 978-1-63807-416-8 | eBook 978-1-63807-184-6
R0

To my two favorite boys, without whom I would have a sparkling clean kitchen always!

CONTENTS

CHANA MASALA, page 28

INTRODUCTION

Indians are well known for our desire to treat our guests with the utmost care and hospitality, and one common way we all seem to do so is through our food. Food holds a very special place in any Indian household. No celebration is complete without a table laden with colorful dishes from end to end, large enough to please royalty.

And though a love of food is passed down between generations, the food itself and the way we make it changes. There are many differences between the way my mom and I come up with our creations. The taste might be very similar, but the way in which we cook is definitely not. My mom likes to use the traditional way, even if it means spending a huge chunk of the day to prep and cook for dinner. And don't get me started on when we have one of those lavish dinner parties!

I, on the other hand, love to find the shortest and easiest routes to get to my destination. I try to make my already busy life a little bit simpler by having a food processor in close proximity, instead of pounding the life out of my mortar and pestle. I also regularly use my Instant Pot, which drastically reduces the amount of time I spend in the kitchen. There are many shortcuts you can use that, when put together, make cooking Indian food a breeze. And I will teach you these tips and shortcuts. Even if you're a believer of the old, traditional ways of cooking, I encourage you to try out my recipes. You'll see that they are loaded with the same flavors.

If you're new to cooking everyday Indian food, you only need to familiarize yourself with a few spices and the flavor combinations that pair well with them. We'll talk more about this in chapter 1. When you're starting out, it's often very easy to lose yourself in the wide selection of spices readily available at grocery stores nowadays. While some of the spices may seem intimidating at first, as you slowly acquaint yourself with the varied flavors they have to offer, you'll soon get excited at the prospect of shopping and stocking your cabinets with some of your very own favorites. Indian food adds a variety of flavors to your palate and can easily be adapted to vegans, as well as vegetarians and meat lovers. This adaptability is a main reason why Indian-inspired menus at dinner parties are well received.

Although India has always had a dominant vegetarian population, veganism has started to see a considerable growth in the last few years. I've been getting a lot of requests recently from some of my readers asking me for vegan variations on some of the classic vegetarian recipes that call for the use of dairy, which is why I decided to put together a collection of recipes custom curated and adapted for cooks who want to eat Indian food that's entirely plant-based.

In this book, you will find plenty of recipes to suit your every need—from simple, quick everyday meals to crowd-pleasers and special festive dishes, as well as classic, popular restaurant favorites. All these recipes have been adapted to the Instant Pot so that you can enjoy the ease of cooking, as well as cleanup, by doing everything in one magical pot. I hope you enjoy cooking and eating these dishes as much as I've enjoyed creating them especially for you.

SAAG PANEER, page 82

CHAPTER ONE

THE VEGAN INDIAN KITCHEN

India is a hugely diverse country, and this is evident in its food as well as in its people. If you traveled throughout all of India, starting from the northernmost point in the province of Kashmir and slowly descending south, making a pit stop in every major city, you would be pleasantly surprised by the variety of food along the way. While this book can't possibly cover every style from the vast subcontinent, I've tried to be as regionally inclusive as possible in my dishes.

Since a large majority of the Indian population is mainly vegetarian, there is no dearth of options for anyone following a vegan diet. In addition to the huge collection of Indian recipes that are already plant-based, there are plenty of others that can be easily altered to be vegan. You'll find 80 such recipes in the pages that follow. In this chapter, however, I'll cover the staples, spices, and pantry items you'll need to get started, as well as how to best use the Instant Pot when cooking Indian food.

THE INDIAN PANTRY

If you're new to Indian cooking and the spice aisles at the local Indian or Asian grocery store intimidate you, don't fret: Just begin with the basics. Here's a list of ingredients that you'll need to make the recipes in this book; they will help you cook many delicious Indian meals any time you want. Have these on hand, and you'll be set for success in your kitchen.

SPICES AND HERBS

Here are some of the most commonly used spices and herbs found in an Indian pantry. Most of these spices are readily available at major grocery stores and can be bought in packs of varying weight. Make sure to store them in a cool, dry place away from any direct heat to prevent them from losing flavor.

Must-Haves

Black peppercorns: Whole peppercorns are commonly added to slow-simmering curries along with other whole spices to infuse them with a blend of aromatic flavors.

Cinnamon sticks: Cinnamon sticks are commonly used to flavor curries, soups, and sweets. When added to curries, they give off a woody, incense-like aroma. These are for flavoring and should not be bitten into.

Cumin seeds: Whole cumin seeds are most often added at the beginning of the cooking process to hot oil. This is called tempering and infuses flavor.

Green cardamom pods: Green cardamom has a slightly sweet aroma and taste. Although it is a popular spice used to flavor Indian curries, it is also commonly found in Indian desserts. The seeds of the cardamom pod are added to spiced Indian tea (chai) while it brews.

Ground coriander: Ground coriander is made by dry roasting whole coriander seeds and grinding them finely. It pairs wonderfully with ground cumin.

Ground cumin: Ground cumin adds a soft, smoky flavor while cooking. It pairs perfectly with ground coriander, and they are often used together.

Ground red chili (cayenne): Red chili powder is made by finely grinding dried red chiles. At major chain grocery stores, this spice is often called cayenne.

Ground turmeric: Although it lacks a spicy flavor per se, turmeric has always been used in Indian cooking for its medicinal and ayurvedic properties. A little goes a long way with turmeric, and adding too much of it can give food a slightly bitter taste, so be conservative when adding.

Mustard seeds: The black mustard seeds used in Indian cooking differ in taste from yellow mustard seeds and have a stronger flavor.

Salt: Table salt is most commonly used in Indian cooking and should be added according to your taste preferences.

Whole cloves: Cloves impart a robust aroma and a strong, spicy flavor to a dish. They are also one of the main flavor enhancers in chai.

Nice-to-Haves

These spices are optional, but they are nice to have since they add complexity to dishes and great value to your Indian pantry.

Black salt: Black salt, also known as Himalayan rock salt or kala namak, is often used in North India as a popular seasoning for fresh-cut fruits and salads.

Curry leaves: Curry leaves are often tempered in oil to soften and release their characteristic flavor in a dish. If you can't find fresh, frozen is often available, or you can leave them out.

Kasoori methi: Kasoori methi is dried fenugreek leaves that can be found at any Indian grocery store. It has a subtle pleasant aroma and gives a unique flavor when added to curries.

Saffron: Derived from the flower of the saffron crocus, these long red threads are used for coloring and seasoning foods. Because saffron is one of the most expensive spices by weight, only a very small amount is ever used at one time.

Masalas

These spice blends are what make Indian curries distinct from other Asian cuisines. Traditionally, these spice blends were freshly ground at home right before use to ensure freshness and maximum flavor while cooking. But nowadays, you can usually find these spices at any Indian grocery store, as well as in most major chain supermarkets. Common spice blends include:

Amchur powder: Also known as dried mango powder, amchur adds a strong tangy flavor while cooking. If you are unable to find it, you can substitute fresh lemon juice at the end of the cooking process.

Chaat masala: A salty-sour spice blend that is usually sprinkled on top of fresh-cut fruit or deep-fried snacks like pakoras to give them an extra edge in flavor.

Garam masala: A robust powdered blend of spices that includes cinnamon, cloves, cumin, peppercorns, and a few others. The color and taste in store-bought garam masala often varies depending on the kinds of spices and amounts used.

Paanch phoron: This is a Bengali spice blend and adds a nice depth of flavor when used in dal or curry recipes.

Tandoori masala: This spice blend is most popularly used in marinades while making grilled tikkas and tandoori dishes.

If you'd like to make your own versions of these common masalas, I include recipes in chapter 7 for Garam Masala (page 110), Tandoori Masala (page 111), and Paanch Phoron (page 112).

SHOPPING FOR YOUR INDIAN PANTRY

When it comes to creating an Indian pantry, keep in mind that a cheaper way to shop for most ingredients is to buy them in bulk from your local Indian or ethnic grocery store. Although you will find that they are readily available at major supermarkets, many of the spices, as well as good-quality basmati rice, will end up costing you at least three times more in price. If you don't have access to an Indian grocer, I've included some online suggestions in the Resources section (page 116) for where to find certain ingredients.

LENTILS AND OTHER LEGUMES

Lentils play an integral role in an Indian meal. They are usually sold dried in prepackaged bags or boxes, but can also be bought in bulk. When you're buying lentils and beans, it is important to keep in mind how much effort you are actually willing to spend in their cooking process. Dried beans like chickpeas and kidney beans taste best when they're soaked overnight and have enough time to soften. While using the Instant Pot does speed up the cooking process, if using dried beans, they should still be soaked for 2 hours in hot water. Using canned beans and legumes is another option, and one that reduces cooking time as well.

The following are the lentils and other legumes you'll see repeatedly used in this book's recipes.

Black-eyed peas: Black-eyed peas are also known as lobia in India and are typically used in the dried form, so they will need to be pre-soaked before cooking. However, using canned black-eyed peas is a great alternative.

Black lentils: These lentils take a fairly long time to cook, and they are the main ingredient in the classic dish Dal Makhani (page 76).

Brown chickpeas: Also called kala chana, brown chickpeas have a nuttier, earthier taste compared to white chickpeas. When the skins are removed and they are split, you get chana dal.

Brown masoor lentils: Also called sabut masoor, these lentils are essentially the whole version of split red lentils. Unlike red lentils, masoor lentils hold their shape better, especially in pressure cookers.

Chana dal: Chana dal, also known as Bengal gram or split brown chickpeas, tend to look like a smaller version of a chickpea cut in half. They are much more robust in flavor than whole chickpeas, however, and are a favorite addition to serve at dinner parties.

Red kidney beans: Just like chickpeas, these beans, also called rajma, need to be pre-soaked. However, using canned kidney beans is a great alternative.

Red lentils: Red lentils, also called masoor, are commonly used in Indian homes since they take the shortest time to cook and require no pre-soaking.

White chickpeas: Dried white chickpeas cook best when they are soaked for 6 to 8 hours. When in a pinch, you can soak them in hot water for 1 to 2 hours and increase your cook time, or simply use canned versions instead.

Whole moong lentils: These look like tiny beans and are green in color.

Yellow lentils: Yellow lentils, also called toor dal or pigeon peas, are usually the base for South Indian specialties like Sambhar (page 20).

Yellow moong lentils: When you split a whole moong lentil, the small yellow moong lentil is what's inside. Also called moong dal and yellow split mung beans, they are used to make Moong Dal Halwa (page 92).

The following is a table of Instant Pot cook times for some of the most common dried beans and lentils used in Indian cooking. These cook times assume they have not been pre-soaked.

Legumes and Rice

LEGUME OR RICE	LIQUID PER 1 CUP OF LEGUME OR GRAIN	MINUTES UNDER PRESSURE	PRESSURE LEVEL	RELEASE
Basmati rice	1½ cups	3	High	Natural for 10 minutes, then Quick
Black-eyed peas	2 cups	30	High	Natural for 10 minutes, then Quick
Brown lentils	1½ cups	10	High	Natural for 10 minutes, then Quick
Chana dal	1½ cups	8	High	Natural for 10 minutes, then Quick
Chickpeas, white and brown	2 cups	30	High	Natural for 10 minutes, then Quick
Green moong lentils	1½ cups	8	High	Natural for 10 minutes, then Quick
Red kidney beans	2 cups	30	High	Natural for 10 minutes, then Quick
Red lentils	1½ cups	3	High	Natural for 10 minutes, then Quick
Yellow lentils	1½ cups	5	High	Natural for 10 minutes, then Quick
Yellow moong lentils	3 cups	5	High	Natural for 10 minutes, then Quick

AROMATICS AND FRESH HERBS

Fresh herbs like cilantro and mint are regularly used in Indian cooking as a garnish. They also add a pop of color and texture to the dish, along with a fresh flavor. These herbs, along with fresh aromatic ingredients like ginger, garlic, and dried chiles, are also commonly blended with various spices to create rich and robust chutneys.

Indian cooking generally calls for fresh herbs to be used as a garnish, and substituting the fresh herbs with dried versions won't give you the desired outcome. If you're missing the fresh herbs like cilantro or mint leaves for the garnishing, I'd suggest simply leaving them out altogether.

OTHER INGREDIENTS

Other pantry staples widely used in Indian cooking include basmati rice, coconut milk, and yogurt. (Using vegan versions of yogurt works just fine. More on that on page 9.) With the following items readily stocked in your pantry or refrigerator, you will be ready to create a wide variety of recipes with what you have on hand.

Basmati rice: Basmati rice is a flavorful long-grain Indian rice generally sold in large bags of 5 to 10 pounds each, but can also be found in smaller, more economical sizes. When cooked properly, each grain remains separate from the others without sticking together.

Canned coconut milk: Canned coconut milk is a great addition to the pantry. It helps make rich, creamy curries.

Chickpea flour (besan): Chickpea flour, commonly called besan in India, is widely used in Indian cooking in recipes like kadhi and pakoras.

Chutneys: Chutneys are spicy condiments made of fruits or vegetables that combine vinegar, spices, and sugar to complement just about any dish. They are easy to make at home. Mint Chutney (page 104), Tomato Chutney (page 103), and Mango Chutney (page 102) take just minutes to make.

Semolina: Semolina, also known as sooji, is basically a form of durum wheat and is often used for making Sooji Halwa (page 91).

Spinach: Fresh or frozen spinach is a great staple to have for a variety of recipes, including Saag Paneer (page 82), Chana Saag (page 34), and Palak Dal (page 19).

Tamarind: Tamarind is typically used in South Indian recipes as a souring agent. While traditionally the recipes often call for the use of tamarind juice, you can easily use store-bought tamarind concentrate as a substitute.

Textured soy protein: While not a traditional Indian staple, if you want to create vegan versions of dishes that involve ground meat, like Keema Matar (page 79) and Keema Pulao (page 83), having textured soy protein on hand is helpful in giving the dish a similar texture and mouthfeel.

Tomatoes, fresh or canned: Fresh tomatoes are preferred when cooking Indian food, but canned tomatoes also work well in curry recipes if you don't have fresh on hand.

Tomato paste: Adding tomato paste into curries intensifies the flavor and adds a nice texture.

INSTANT POT AND INDIAN COOKING

Most Indian cooking does not really require any special equipment. However, a pressure cooker has been an integral part of an Indian kitchen for ages, as it saves time and energy. Compared to older pressure cookers, which would hiss every few minutes with their loud whistles and risk bursting open when even slightly overfilled, many Indian cooks have opted to use the safer, quieter, and more versatile Instant Pot. From lentils to slow-cooked dried beans and curries, an Instant Pot is a great addition to the Indian kitchen.

With the Instant Pot you have the option to cook a variety of recipes, including curries and vegetable stir-fries, flavored rice-based meals, and even desserts. The Instant Pot is great for cooking classic recipes like Chana Masala (page 28) and Rajma (page 16), where you don't necessarily want to pre-soak chickpeas or kidney beans overnight. Adjusting the cooking time on the Instant Pot while using these beans in their dried form will ensure you get the best possible results in a fraction of the time.

Vegan Ingredient Substitutes

Since a large part of the Indian population follows a strict vegetarian diet, dairy plays an important role in the cuisine. Many traditional vegetarian recipes call for the addition of dairy products such as milk, cream, and paneer. These ingredients, however, can be easily substituted with vegan options today and are just as tasty.

Cream: When trying to substitute cream with a vegan option in a traditional Indian recipe, finely ground cashew or almond pastes work extremely well. They give a similar texture and color to the recipe that is desired from the addition of a dairy-based cream. You can also use coconut cream (the solid part at the top of the coconut milk can).

Ghee: Most traditional Indian recipes call for the use of ghee, but these can easily be adapted by using various cooking oils instead. Neutral oils such as avocado, canola, peanut, and corn oil work well since they can withstand the higher temperatures and longer cooking times that are often called for in Indian cooking.

Milk: Coconut milk is most often an excellent substitute for dairy milk in many Indian recipes. It imparts a slightly sweet flavor and won't curdle, unlike most nut-based milks, during the cooking process.

Paneer: Paneer is widely used as a meat substitute for vegetarians in Indian cuisine and can be swapped with tofu for a vegan option. Although tofu does have a slightly more pronounced flavor when compared to paneer, the spices in Indian recipes help eliminate it without drastically altering the end result.

Yogurt: There are tons of high-quality vegan yogurt options readily available these days. Options include yogurt from oats, soy, coconut, and even tofu, and many of them work extremely well as a substitute in traditional Indian recipes. You may have to experiment with different brands to find what works best for you, taste-wise.

Tips for Instant Pot Success

Here are a few tips to ensure success when cooking with the Instant Pot:

- Never fill your Instant Pot over the maximum line given. This will prevent your food from spilling and causing any accidents.

- Always make sure to deglaze the bottom of the pot if you see that the food starts to stick, to avoid scorching the pot and to prevent your food from burning. Deglazing involves scraping up the browned bits of food using a wooden spoon or other utensil and a splash of water.

- Make sure that there is enough liquid in the pot to cook the food. If the food looks a bit too dry, add in some water to prevent the food from burning.

- Always make sure to set the valve to the sealing position before setting your pressure cook timer.

- When releasing the pressure manually, always keep in mind that steam will escape from the pressure valve quite rapidly—so keep your hands and face away from the steam valve during release to avoid getting hurt.

- If you live at a high altitude, you'll have to adjust the cooking times because of the difference in atmospheric pressure. A general rule of thumb is to increase pressure time by 5 percent for every 1,000 feet above 2,000 feet. For instance, if a dish cooks under pressure for 20 minutes at sea level, then it would cook for 21 minutes at 3,000 feet, and 23 minutes at 5,000 feet above sea level.

FLAVOR-BUILDING TECHNIQUES

There are a few cooking techniques that are mainly pertinent to Indian cooking. Although these techniques are traditionally meant for stove-top cooking, they can be adapted to the Instant Pot by using the Sauté function at the maximum heat level.

TOASTING SPICES

Dry roasting whole spices helps bring out their essential oils and intensifies their flavors and aromas when added to the food. Make sure to keep stirring the spices constantly to keep them from burning.

TADKA

Tadka is the process of heating oil and flavoring it with spices like whole cumin seeds, mustard seeds, and dried chiles. This warm oil is then added to cooked dal to give it an extra burst of flavor right before serving.

BHUNAO

This is a typical technique in Indian cooking that basically consists of sautéing spices with aromatics like onions, ginger, and/or garlic to ensure that the flavors are well penetrated throughout the dish.

ABOUT THE RECIPES

The recipes I've selected for this book work extremely well for the Instant Pot. I've tried to include recipes that are most commonly cooked in Indian homes in addition to popular restaurant favorites that represent as many cooking traditions and regions of India as possible.

I've used a 6-quart Instant Pot for all the recipes, which is the perfect size to cook for 4 to 6 people. However, these recipes can be easily adapted to a larger size Instant Pot, as well as more people, if desired.

For greater meal planning ease, I've included the time the Instant Pot takes to come under pressure, in addition to prep time and time cooked under pressure. Where appropriate, I've also included the time it takes to naturally release pressure, so you have an accurate idea of how long a dish will take from start to finish.

For ease of use and to accommodate possible allergies, the recipes indicate whether a recipe is Nut-Free, Gluten-Free, or Soy-Free. The Super Fast label notes when a recipe takes 30 minutes or less to make, including prep and cook time.

Many recipes also include one of the following tips:

Prep Tip: This involves a shortcut or advice on how to ensure a recipe's success.

Ingredient Tip: This is for unusual or uncommon ingredients not mentioned in chapter 1. It may also suggest a substitute, even if it's not an exact substitute for the flavor.

Variation: This involves a simple swap that increases the versatility of the dish and gives it a different flavor profile.

CHANA MASALA, page 28

CHAPTER TWO

....

DALS AND BEAN DISHES

RAJMA (RED KIDNEY BEAN CURRY)

GLUTEN-FREE, NUT-FREE, SOY-FREE

Prep time: 10 minutes **Sauté time:** 8 minutes **Pressure build:** 8 to 10 minutes
Pressure cook: 30 minutes **Pressure release:** Natural, 10 to 12 minutes
Total time: 1 hour, 10 minutes **Serves 4**

This red kidney bean curry is a favorite in many homes in Northern India and is perfect for an easy, hearty weeknight meal. It is usually served with a side of Perfect Basmati Rice (page 42) and a chopped salad for a simple and well-balanced meal.

2 tablespoons neutral cooking oil

1 cinnamon stick

1 teaspoon cumin seeds

1 large onion, finely chopped

1 tablespoon finely minced garlic

1 tablespoon finely minced ginger

2 tablespoons tomato paste

1 tablespoon ground coriander

½ teaspoon ground red chili

½ teaspoon Garam Masala (page 110)

Salt

2 medium tomatoes, finely chopped

3 cups water

2 (15-ounce) cans red kidney beans, drained and rinsed (if using dried, soak 1½ cups beans for 2 hours in hot water)

Fresh cilantro leaves, for garnish

1. Select Sauté mode, adjust the heat to high, and put the oil, cinnamon stick, and cumin seeds in the Instant Pot.

2. Once the cumin seeds start to sizzle, add the onion, garlic, and ginger and cook for 3 to 4 minutes, until the onion begins to brown. Keep stirring occasionally to avoid burning.

3. Add the tomato paste, coriander, red chili, and garam masala and season with salt. Mix well.

4. Slowly add the tomatoes and cook for 3 to 4 minutes, until they start to pulp and blend in with the spices.

5. Add the water and kidney beans and stir well to combine.

6. Turn off Sauté mode, lock the lid, and close the steam valve. Press Manual and set the timer for 20 minutes on high pressure for canned beans or 30 minutes on high pressure for dried beans.

7. When the timer goes off, let the pressure release naturally for 10 to 12 minutes, then quick release any remaining pressure. Carefully remove the lid.

8. Garnish with finely chopped cilantro and serve warm.

Per serving: Calories: 276; Total fat: 9g; Saturated fat: 1g; Sodium: 299mg; Carbohydrates: 39g; Sugar: 10g; Fiber: 9g; Protein: 13g; Calcium: 108mg

CHOLE (CHICKPEA CURRY)

GLUTEN-FREE, NUT-FREE, SOY-FREE

Prep time: 10 minutes **Sauté time:** 8 minutes **Pressure build:** 8 to 10 minutes
Pressure cook: 30 minutes **Pressure release:** Natural, 10 to 12 minutes
Total time: 1 hour, 10 minutes **Serves 4**

In many parts of India, chole is a very popular street food served alongside deep-fried bread called bhature. Chole-Bhature is usually enjoyed as a weekend brunch but pairing this dish with a side of rice or naan would make it a great lunch option.

2 tablespoons neutral cooking oil
1 teaspoon cumin seeds
1 large onion, finely chopped
1 tablespoon finely minced garlic
1 tablespoon finely minced ginger
2 tablespoons tomato paste
1 tablespoon ground coriander
½ teaspoon ground red chili
½ teaspoon Garam Masala (page 110)
¼ teaspoon ground turmeric
Salt
2 medium tomatoes, finely chopped
3 cups water
2 (15-ounce) cans chickpeas, drained and rinsed (if using dried, soak 1½ cups for 2 hours in hot water)
Fresh cilantro leaves

1. Select Sauté mode, adjust the heat to high, and put the oil and cumin seeds in the Instant Pot.

2. Once the cumin seeds start to sizzle, add the onion, garlic, and ginger and cook for 3 to 4 minutes, until the onion begins to brown. Keep stirring occasionally to avoid burning.

3. Add the tomato paste, coriander, red chili, garam masala, and turmeric and season with salt. Mix well.

4. Slowly add the tomatoes and cook for 3 to 4 minutes, until they start to pulp and blend in with the spices.

5. Add the water and chickpeas and stir well to combine.

6. Turn off Sauté mode, lock the lid, and close the steam valve. Press Manual and set the timer for 20 minutes on high pressure for canned chickpeas or 30 minutes on high pressure for dried chickpeas.

7. When the timer goes off, let the pressure release naturally for 10 to 12 minutes, then quick release any remaining pressure. Carefully remove the lid.

8. Garnish with finely chopped cilantro and serve warm.

PREP TIP: If you have the time, use dried chickpeas pre-soaked for at least 6 hours for best results.

Per serving: Calories: 290; Total fat: 11g; Saturated fat: 1g; Sodium: 294mg; Carbohydrates: 39g; Sugar: 10g; Fiber: 10g; Protein: 11g; Calcium: 89mg

ALU CHANA (CHICKPEAS AND POTATO CURRY)

GLUTEN-FREE, NUT-FREE, SOY-FREE

Prep time: 10 minutes **Sauté time:** 8 minutes **Pressure build:** 8 to 10 minutes
Pressure cook: 30 minutes **Pressure release:** Natural, 10 to 12 minutes
Total time: 1 hour, 10 minutes **Serves 4**

This simple dish of chickpeas and potatoes cooked together in a mild curry is an absolute comfort food. Pair it with a side of Perfect Basmati Rice (page 42) and a salad for a complete, well-balanced meal.

2 tablespoons neutral cooking oil
1 teaspoon cumin seeds
1 large onion, finely chopped
1 tablespoon finely minced garlic
1 tablespoon finely minced ginger
½ teaspoon ground red chili
¼ teaspoon ground turmeric
1 tablespoon ground coriander
½ teaspoon Garam Masala (page 110)
Salt
2 medium tomatoes, finely chopped
3 cups water
2 medium potatoes, quartered
2 (15-ounce) cans chickpeas, drained and rinsed (if using dried, soak 1½ cups for 2 hours in hot water)
Fresh cilantro leaves

1. Select Sauté mode, adjust the heat to high, and put the oil and cumin seeds in the Instant Pot.

2. Once the cumin seeds start to sizzle, add the onion, garlic, and ginger and cook for 3 to 4 minutes, until the onion begins to brown. Keep stirring occasionally to avoid burning.

3. Add the red chili, turmeric, coriander, and garam masala and season with salt. Mix well.

4. Slowly add the tomatoes and cook for 3 to 4 minutes, until they start to pulp and blend in with the spices.

5. Add the water, potatoes, and chickpeas and stir well to combine.

6. Turn off Sauté mode, lock the lid, and close the steam valve. Press Manual and set the timer for 20 minutes on high pressure for canned chickpeas or 30 minutes on high pressure for dried chickpeas.

7. When the timer goes off, let the pressure release naturally for 10 to 12 minutes, then quick release any remaining pressure. Carefully remove the lid.

8. Garnish with finely chopped cilantro and serve warm.

Per serving: Calories: 357; Total fat: 11g; Saturated fat: 1g; Sodium: 306mg; Carbohydrates: 55g; Sugar: 10g; Fiber: 13g; Protein: 12g; Calcium: 96mg

PALAK DAL (SPINACH DAL)

GLUTEN-FREE, NUT-FREE, SOY-FREE

Prep time: 10 minutes **Sauté time:** 7 minutes **Pressure build:** 8 to 10 minutes
Pressure cook: 8 minutes **Pressure release:** Natural, 10 to 12 minutes
Total time: 47 minutes **Serves 4**

This green moong lentil dish cooked with spinach is perfect on cold winter nights served alongside some crusty bread as a soup, or paired with rice the traditional way.

2 tablespoons neutral cooking oil
1 teaspoon cumin seeds
1 medium onion, finely chopped
1 tablespoon finely minced garlic
1 tablespoon finely minced ginger
1 teaspoon ground coriander
½ teaspoon ground red chili
¼ teaspoon ground turmeric
Salt
1 large tomato, finely chopped
3 cups finely chopped fresh spinach
2 cups dried green moong lentils, rinsed and drained
2 cups water

1. Select Sauté mode, adjust the heat to high, and put the oil and cumin seeds in the Instant Pot.

2. Once the cumin seeds start to sizzle, add the onion, garlic, and ginger and cook for 3 to 4 minutes, until the onion begins to brown. Keep stirring occasionally to avoid burning.

3. Add the coriander, red chili, and turmeric and season with salt. Mix well.

4. Slowly add the tomato and cook for 2 to 3 minutes, until it starts to pulp and blend in with the spices.

5. Add the spinach, green moong lentils, and water and stir well to combine.

6. Turn off Sauté mode, lock the lid, and close the steam valve. Press Manual and set the timer for 8 minutes on high pressure.

7. When the timer goes off, let the pressure release naturally for 10 to 12 minutes, then quick release any remaining pressure. Carefully remove the lid.

8. Serve warm.

Per serving: Calories: 435; Total fat: 8g; Saturated fat: 1g; Sodium: 43mg; Carbohydrates: 67g; Sugar: 3g; Fiber: 16g; Protein: 26g; Calcium: 160mg

SAMBHAR (SOUTH INDIAN LENTIL STEW)

GLUTEN-FREE, NUT-FREE, SOY-FREE

Prep time: 10 minutes **Sauté time:** 6 minutes **Pressure build:** 8 to 10 minutes
Pressure cook: 5 minutes **Pressure release:** Natural, 8 to 10 minutes
Total time: 41 minutes **Serves 4**

Sambhar is a traditional tangy and spicy lentil soup from South India made with a variety of seasonal vegetables. It is mostly paired with crepes called dosas or steamed rice cakes called idlis.

2 tablespoons neutral cooking oil
1 teaspoon mustard seeds
1 medium onion, finely chopped
6 or 7 fresh curry leaves
1 tablespoon finely minced garlic
1 tablespoon finely minced ginger
2 tablespoons sambhar masala powder
Salt
1 large tomato, finely chopped
2 cups dried yellow lentils, rinsed and drained
2 cups water
1 teaspoon tamarind paste
Fresh cilantro leaves finely chopped, for garnish

1. Select Sauté mode, adjust the heat to high, and put the oil and mustard seeds in the Instant Pot.

2. Once the mustard seeds start to sizzle, add the onion, curry leaves, garlic, and ginger and cook for 2 to 3 minutes, until the onion begins to brown. Keep stirring occasionally to avoid burning.

3. Add the sambhar masala and season with salt. Mix well.

4. Slowly add the tomato and cook for 2 to 3 minutes, until it starts to pulp and blend in with the spices.

5. Add the lentils, water, and tamarind paste and stir well to combine.

6. Turn off Sauté mode, lock the lid, and close the steam valve. Press Manual and set the timer for 5 minutes on high pressure.

7. When the timer goes off, let the pressure release naturally for 8 to 10 minutes, then quick release any remaining pressure. Carefully remove the lid.

8. Garnish with cilantro and serve warm.

Per serving: Calories: 480; Total fat: 9g; Saturated fat: 1g; Sodium: 5mg; Carbohydrates: 76g; Sugar: 5g; Fiber: 16g; Protein: 27g; Calcium: 74mg

½ can coconut milk
More spice

DAL TADKA

GLUTEN-FREE, NUT-FREE, SOY-FREE

Prep time: 10 minutes **Sauté time:** 6 minutes **Pressure build:** 8 to 10 minutes
Pressure cook: 3 minutes **Pressure release:** Natural, 8 to 10 minutes
Total time: 39 minutes **Serves 4**

This is a very popular recipe consisting of lentils flavored simply with fried onions and spices. This recipe is a personal favorite of mine for **busy days since** the lentils are really quick to cook.

2 tablespoons neutral
  cooking oil
1 teaspoon cumin seeds
1 medium onion,
  finely chopped
1 tablespoon finely
  minced ginger
½ teaspoon ground
  red chili
½ teaspoon ground
  coriander
¼ teaspoon ground
  turmeric
Salt
1 medium tomato,
  finely chopped
2 cups dried red lentils,
  rinsed and drained
1½ cups water
Fresh cilantro leaves,
  finely chopped,
  for garnish

1. Select Sauté mode, adjust the heat to high, and put the oil and cumin seeds in the Instant Pot.

2. Once the cumin seeds start to sizzle, add the onion and ginger and cook for 2 to 3 minutes, until the onion begins to brown. Keep stirring occasionally to avoid burning.

3. Add the red chili, coriander, and turmeric and season with salt. Mix well.

4. Slowly add the tomato and cook for 2 to 3 minutes, until it starts to pulp and blend in with the spices.

5. Add the lentils and water and stir well to combine.

6. Turn off Sauté mode, lock the lid, and close the steam valve. Press Manual and set the timer for 3 minutes on high pressure.

7. When the timer goes off, let the pressure release naturally for 8 to 10 minutes, then quick release any remaining pressure. Carefully remove the lid.

8. Garnish with cilantro and serve warm.

Per serving: Calories: 423; Total fat: 9g; Saturated fat: 1g; Sodium: 14mg; Carbohydrates: 61g; Sugar: 4g; Fiber: 15g; Protein: 27g; Calcium: 56mg

CHANA DAL MASALA

GLUTEN-FREE, NUT-FREE, SOY-FREE

Prep time: 10 minutes **Sauté time:** 6 minutes **Pressure build:** 8 to 10 minutes
Pressure cook: 6 minutes **Pressure release:** Natural, 8 to 10 minutes
Total time: 42 minutes **Serves 4**

Chana dal masala takes dried chana dal and cooks it down to a tender consistency.
It's flavored with sautéed onions, ginger, garlic, and a bunch of spices.

2 tablespoons neutral
 cooking oil
1 teaspoon cumin seeds
1 teaspoon fennel seeds
1 medium onion, finely
 chopped
1 tablespoon finely
 minced garlic
1 tablespoon finely
 minced ginger
1 tablespoon
 tomato paste
1 teaspoon ground
 coriander
½ teaspoon ground
 red chili
¼ teaspoon ground
 turmeric
Salt
1 large tomato, finely
 chopped
2 cups dried chana
 dal lentils, rinsed
 and drained
2 cups water
Fresh cilantro leaves,
 finely chopped,
 for garnish

1. Select Sauté mode, adjust the heat to high, and
 put the oil, cumin seeds, and fennel seeds in the
 Instant Pot.

2. Once the cumin and fennel seeds start to sizzle,
 add the onion, garlic, and ginger and cook for 2 to
 3 minutes, until the onion begins to brown. Keep
 stirring occasionally to avoid burning.

3. Add the tomato paste, coriander, red chili, and
 turmeric and season with salt. Mix well.

4. Slowly add the tomato and cook for 2 to 3 minutes,
 until it starts to pulp and blend in with the spices.

5. Add the lentils and water and stir well to combine.

6. Turn off Sauté mode, lock the lid, and close the
 steam valve. Press Manual and set the timer for
 6 minutes on high pressure.

7. When the timer goes off, let the pressure release
 naturally for 8 to 10 minutes, then quick release any
 remaining pressure. Carefully remove the lid.

8. Garnish with cilantro and serve warm.

Per serving: Calories: 395; Total fat: 10g; Saturated fat: 1g;
Sodium: 8mg; Carbohydrates: 63g; Sugar: 5g; Fiber: 24g;
Protein: 15g; Calcium: 186mg

KALI DAL (CURRIED BLACK LENTILS)

GLUTEN-FREE, NUT-FREE, SOY-FREE

Prep time: 10 minutes **Sauté time:** 6 minutes **Pressure build:** 8 to 10 minutes
Pressure cook: 10 minutes **Pressure release:** Natural, 8 to 10 minutes
Total time: 46 minutes **Serves 4**

This simple homestyle black lentil curry is made with whole spices and is pure comfort food. This is a much simpler and healthier version of the restaurant-style Dal Makhani (page 76) and is best enjoyed with some fresh baked naan and kebabs.

2 tablespoons neutral cooking oil
1 teaspoon cumin seeds
1 medium onion, finely chopped
1 tablespoon finely minced garlic
1 tablespoon finely minced ginger
1 tablespoon tomato paste
1 tablespoon ground coriander
½ teaspoon ground red chili
Salt
1 large tomato, finely chopped
2 cups dried whole black lentils, rinsed and drained
2 cups water
Fresh cilantro leaves, finely chopped, for garnish

1. Select Sauté mode, adjust the heat to high, and put the oil and cumin seeds in the Instant Pot.

2. Once the cumin seeds start to sizzle, add the onion, garlic, and ginger and cook for 2 to 3 minutes, until the onion begins to brown. Keep stirring occasionally to avoid burning.

3. Add the tomato paste, coriander, and red chili and season with salt. Mix well.

4. Slowly add the tomato and cook for 2 to 3 minutes, until it starts to pulp and blend in with the spices.

5. Add the lentils and water and stir well to combine.

6. Turn off Sauté mode, lock the lid, and close the steam valve. Press Manual and set the timer for 10 minutes on high pressure.

7. When the timer goes off, let the pressure release naturally for 8 to 10 minutes, then quick release any remaining pressure. Carefully remove the lid.

8. Garnish with cilantro and serve warm.

Per serving: Calories: 384; Total fat: 9g; Saturated fat: 1g; Sodium: 14mg; Carbohydrates: 57g; Sugar: 5g; Fiber: 21g; Protein: 25g; Calcium: 63mg

LOBIA MASALA (BLACK-EYED PEA CURRY)

GLUTEN-FREE, NUT-FREE, SOY-FREE

Prep time: 10 minutes **Sauté time:** 8 minutes **Pressure build:** 8 to 10 minutes
Pressure cook: 25 minutes **Pressure release:** Natural, 10 to 12 minutes
Total time: 1 hour, 5 minutes **Serves 4**

Lobia masala is a North Indian–style black-eyed pea curry made with a rich gravy base of sautéed onions and tomatoes. This is usually served with warm Indian flatbreads called rotis, and dry vegetable dishes like Achari Gobi (page 62) or Bhindi do Piaza (page 69) on the side.

2 tablespoons neutral cooking oil
1 teaspoon cumin seeds
1 large onion, finely chopped
1 tablespoon finely minced garlic
1 tablespoon finely minced ginger
2 tablespoons tomato paste
1 tablespoon ground coriander
½ teaspoon ground red chili
½ teaspoon amchur powder
¼ teaspoon ground turmeric
Salt
2 medium tomatoes, finely chopped
3 cups water

1. Select Sauté mode, adjust the heat to high, and put the oil and cumin seeds in the Instant Pot.

2. Once the cumin seeds start to sizzle, add the onion, garlic, and ginger and cook for 3 to 4 minutes, until the onion begins to brown. Keep stirring occasionally to avoid burning.

3. Add the tomato paste, coriander, red chili, amchur powder, and turmeric and season with salt. Mix well.

4. Slowly add the tomatoes and cook for 3 to 4 minutes, until they start to pulp and blend in with the spices.

5. Add the water and black-eyed peas and stir well to combine.

6. Turn off Sauté mode, lock the lid, and close the steam valve. Press Manual and set the timer for 20 minutes on high pressure for canned beans or 25 minutes on high pressure for dried beans.

7. When the timer goes off, let the pressure release naturally for 10 to 12 minutes, then quick release any remaining pressure. Carefully remove the lid.

8. Garnish with cilantro and serve warm.

2 (15-ounce) cans
  black-eyed peas,
  drained and rinsed
  (if using dried, soak
  1½ cups for 2 hours in
  hot water)
Fresh cilantro leaves, finely
  chopped, for garnish

PREP TIP: If you have the time, I'd suggest using dried black-eyed peas pre-soaked overnight or at least 6 hours for best results.

Per serving: Calories: 261; Total fat: 9g; Saturated fat: 1g; Sodium: 55mg; Carbohydrates: 37g; Sugar: 6g; Fiber: 9g; Protein: 12g; Calcium: 60mg

MIXED DAL

GLUTEN-FREE, NUT-FREE, SOY-FREE

Prep time: 10 minutes **Sauté time:** 6 minutes **Pressure build:** 8 to 10 minutes
Pressure cook: 8 minutes **Pressure release:** Natural, 10 to 12 minutes
Total time: 46 minutes **Serves 4**

This dal is great when you have a little of everything in your pantry and want to make something quick and wholesome. It pairs great with Perfect Basmati Rice (page 42) and some Kachumber (page 109), or with chutney on the side.

2 tablespoons neutral
    cooking oil
1 teaspoon fennel seeds
1 teaspoon cumin seeds
1 medium onion, finely
    chopped
1 tablespoon finely
    minced garlic
1 teaspoon ground
    coriander
½ teaspoon ground
    red chili
¼ teaspoon ground
    turmeric
Salt
1 large tomato,
    finely chopped
2 cups water

1. Select Sauté mode, adjust the heat to high, and put the oil, fennel seeds, and cumin seeds in the Instant Pot.

2. Once the fennel and cumin seeds start to sizzle, add the onion and garlic and cook for 2 to 3 minutes, until the onion begins to brown. Keep stirring occasionally to avoid burning.

3. Add the coriander, red chili, and turmeric and season with salt. Mix well.

4. Slowly add the tomato and cook for 2 to 3 minutes, until it starts to pulp and blend in with the spices.

5. Add the water, moong lentils, red lentils, and toor lentils and stir well to combine.

6. Turn off Sauté mode, lock the lid, and close the steam valve. Press Manual and set the timer for 8 minutes on high pressure.

½ cup dried green
moong lentils, rinsed
and drained
½ cup dried red lentils,
rinsed and drained
½ cup dried yellow
(toor) lentils, rinsed
and drained
Fresh cilantro leaves,
finely chopped,
for garnish

7. When the timer goes off, let the pressure release naturally for 10 to 12 minutes, then quick release any remaining pressure. Carefully remove the lid.

8. Garnish with cilantro and serve warm.

INGREDIENT TIP: You can mix and match the lentils, depending on what you have in your pantry. Just keep the individual cooking times of each type of lentil you use in mind to gauge the overall cooking time. Adding a mix of quick-cooking and longer-cooking lentils will give your dish great texture.

Per serving: Calories: 343; Total fat: 8g; Saturated fat: 1g; Sodium: 15mg; Carbohydrates: 49g; Sugar: 3g; Fiber: 12g; Protein: 20g; Calcium: 74mg

CHANA MASALA

GLUTEN-FREE, NUT-FREE, SOY-FREE

Prep time: 10 minutes **Sauté time:** 8 minutes **Pressure build:** 8 to 10 minutes
Pressure cook: 30 minutes **Pressure release:** Natural, 10 to 12 minutes
Total time: 1 hour, 10 minutes **Serves 4**

This spicy chickpea curry is a popular restaurant favorite and most commonly eaten with deep-fried puffy bread, called puris, for a hearty weekend brunch. I personally love to have this with a side of Jeera Rice (page 44) and some Kachumber (page 109).

2 tablespoons neutral
  cooking oil
1 teaspoon cumin seeds
1 large onion, finely
  chopped
1 tablespoon finely
  minced garlic
1 tablespoon finely
  minced ginger
2 tablespoons
  tomato paste
1 tablespoon ground
  coriander
½ teaspoon ground
  red chili
½ teaspoon Garam
  Masala (page 110)
½ teaspoon
  amchur powder
¼ teaspoon ground
  turmeric
Salt
2 medium tomatoes,
  finely chopped
3 cups water
2 (15-ounce) cans
  chickpeas, drained
  and rinsed (if using
  dried, soak 1½ cups for
  2 hours in hot water)
Fresh cilantro leaves

1. Select Sauté mode, adjust the heat to high, and put the oil and cumin seeds in the Instant Pot.

2. Once the cumin seeds start to sizzle, add the onion, garlic, and ginger and cook for 3 to 4 minutes, until the onion begins to brown. Keep stirring occasionally to avoid burning.

3. Add the tomato paste, coriander, red chili, garam masala, amchur powder, and turmeric and season with salt. Mix well.

4. Slowly add the tomatoes and cook for 3 to 4 minutes, until they start to pulp and blend in with the spices.

5. Add the water and chickpeas and stir well to combine.

6. Turn off Sauté mode, lock the lid, and close the steam valve. Press Manual and set the timer for 20 minutes on high pressure for canned chickpeas or 30 minutes on high pressure for dried chickpeas.

7. When the timer goes off, let the pressure release naturally for 10 to 12 minutes, then quick release any remaining pressure. Carefully remove the lid.

8. Garnish with finely chopped cilantro and serve warm.

Per serving: Calories: 290; Total fat: 11g; Saturated fat: 1g; Sodium: 294mg; Carbohydrates: 39g; Sugar: 10g; Fiber: 10g; Protein: 11g; Calcium: 91mg

COCONUT CHICKPEA CURRY

GLUTEN-FREE, SOY-FREE

Prep time: 10 minutes **Sauté time:** 3 minutes **Pressure build:** 8 to 10 minutes
Pressure cook: 30 minutes **Pressure release:** Natural, 10 to 12 minutes
Total time: 1 hour, 5 minutes **Serves 4**

This is a mildly spiced coconut-based curry with chickpeas that pairs well with
a side of Perfect Basmati Rice (page 42). Although it is quick and easy to make,
the end result seems like you worked hard on the dish, making this a great recipe
for entertaining!

2 tablespoons neutral
    cooking oil
1 cinnamon stick
3 or 4 whole green
    cardamom pods
1 large onion, thinly sliced
1 tablespoon finely
    minced garlic
1 tablespoon finely
    minced ginger
1 tablespoon ground
    coriander
½ teaspoon ground
    red chili
¼ teaspoon ground
    turmeric
Salt
2 (15-ounce) cans
    chickpeas, drained
    and rinsed (if using
    dried, soak 1½ cups for
    2 hours in hot water)
2 cups water
1 cup full-fat coconut milk
1 large tomato,
    finely chopped
Fresh cilantro leaves,
    finely chopped,
    for garnish

1. Select Sauté mode, adjust the heat to high, and put
   the oil, cinnamon stick, and cardamom pods in the
   Instant Pot.

2. Once the cardamom pods start to sizzle, add the
   onion, garlic, and ginger and cook for 1 to 2 minutes,
   until the onion begins to brown. Keep stirring occasionally to avoid burning.

3. Add the coriander, red chili, and turmeric and season
   with salt. Mix well.

4. Add the chickpeas, water, coconut milk, and tomato
   and stir well to combine.

5. Turn off Sauté mode, lock the lid, and close the
   steam valve. Press Manual and set the timer for
   20 minutes on high pressure for canned chickpeas or
   30 minutes on high pressure for dried chickpeas.

6. When the timer goes off, let the pressure release
   naturally for 10 to 12 minutes, then quick release any
   remaining pressure. Carefully remove the lid.

7. Garnish with cilantro and serve warm.

Per serving: Calories: 381; Total fat: 21g; Saturated fat: 11g;
Sodium: 293mg; Carbohydrates: 40g; Sugar: 10g; Fiber: 10g;
Protein: 11g; Calcium: 83mg

VEGETABLE DAL

GLUTEN-FREE, NUT-FREE, SOY-FREE

Prep time: 10 minutes **Sauté time:** 6 minutes **Pressure build:** 8 to 10 minutes
Pressure cook: 3 minutes **Pressure release:** Natural, 8 to 10 minutes
Total time: 39 minutes **Serves 4**

Inspired by a traditional Parsi dish called dhansak, this vegetable dal is slow cooked with a mix of seasonal vegetables and spices. You can change up the vegetables depending on what's in season and your preference.

2 tablespoons neutral
   cooking oil
1 teaspoon cumin seeds
1 medium onion, finely
   chopped
1 tablespoon finely
   minced garlic
1 tablespoon finely
   minced ginger
1 teaspoon ground
   coriander
½ teaspoon ground
   red chili
¼ teaspoon ground
   turmeric
Salt
1 medium tomato,
   finely chopped
2 cups dried red lentils,
   rinsed and drained
1½ cups water
½ cup finely chopped
   carrots
½ cup finely chopped
   green beans
½ cup frozen
   peas, thawed
Fresh cilantro leaves,
   finely chopped,
   for garnish

1. Select Sauté mode, adjust the heat to high, and put the oil and cumin seeds in the Instant Pot.

2. Once the cumin seeds start to sizzle, add the onion, garlic, and ginger and cook for 2 to 3 minutes, until the onion begins to brown. Keep stirring occasionally to avoid burning.

3. Add the coriander, red chili, and turmeric and season with salt. Mix well.

4. Slowly add the tomato and cook for 2 to 3 minutes, until it starts to pulp and blend in with the spices.

5. Add the lentils, water, carrots, green beans, and peas and stir well to combine.

6. Turn off Sauté mode, lock the lid, and close the steam valve. Press Manual and set the timer for 3 minutes on high pressure.

7. When the timer goes off, let the pressure release naturally for 8 to 10 minutes, then quick release any remaining pressure. Carefully remove the lid.

8. Garnish with cilantro and serve warm.

Per serving: Calories: 451; Total fat: 9g; Saturated fat: 1g; Sodium: 44mg; Carbohydrates: 66g; Sugar: 6g; Fiber: 17g; Protein: 28g; Calcium: 71mg

MASALA MASOOR DAL (SPICED LENTIL CURRY)

GLUTEN-FREE, NUT-FREE, SOY-FREE

Prep time: 10 minutes **Sauté time:** 8 minutes **Pressure build:** 8 to 10 minutes
Pressure cook: 5 minutes **Pressure release:** Natural, 8 to 10 minutes
Total time: 43 minutes **Serves 4**

This is one of the most common everyday dal recipes eaten in many Indian homes. It is simple, quick, and perfect for a busy weeknight. Add in some rice or rotis on the side and a dry vegetable dish like Baingan Bharta (page 65), and you will have a delicious, complete meal.

2 tablespoons neutral cooking oil
1 cinnamon stick
1 teaspoon cumin seeds
1 medium onion, finely chopped
1 tablespoon finely minced garlic
1 tablespoon finely minced ginger
1 teaspoon ground coriander
½ teaspoon ground red chili
¼ teaspoon ground turmeric
¼ teaspoon Garam Masala (page 110)
Salt
1 large tomato, finely chopped
2 cups dried brown masoor lentils, rinsed and drained
2 cups water
Fresh cilantro leaves, finely chopped, for garnish

1. Select Sauté mode, adjust the heat to high, and put the oil, cinnamon stick, and cumin seeds in the Instant Pot.

2. Once the cumin seeds start to sizzle, add the onion, garlic, and ginger and cook for 2 to 3 minutes, until the onion begins to brown. Keep stirring occasionally to avoid burning.

3. Add the coriander, red chili, turmeric, and garam masala and season with salt. Mix well.

4. Slowly add the tomato and cook for 2 to 3 minutes, until it starts to pulp and blend in with the spices.

5. Add the lentils and water and stir well to combine.

6. Turn off Sauté mode, lock the lid, and close the steam valve. Press Manual and set the timer for 5 minutes on high pressure.

7. When the timer goes off, let the pressure release naturally for 8 to 10 minutes, then quick release any remaining pressure. Carefully remove the lid.

8. Garnish with cilantro and serve warm.

Per serving: Calories: 414; Total fat: 7g; Saturated fat: 1g; Sodium: 15mg; Carbohydrates: 60g; Sugar: 2g; Fiber: 29g; Protein: 27g; Calcium: 99mg

KALA CHANA (SPICED BROWN CHICKPEAS)

GLUTEN-FREE, NUT-FREE, SOY-FREE

Prep time: 10 minutes, plus 2 hours' soak time **Sauté time:** 8 minutes **Pressure build:** 8 to 10 minutes **Pressure cook:** 30 minutes **Pressure release:** Natural, 10 to 12 minutes **Total time:** 3 hours, 10 minutes **Serves 4**

This is a wonderful dish to make ahead as the flavors only deepen as it sits. When ready to eat, simply heat it up and garnish with fresh cilantro leaves and a sprinkle of lemon juice. Brown chickpeas, popularly known as kala chana in India, are a variety of chickpea that is a darker brown color and slightly smaller in size. They need to be soaked for 2 hours before cooking, so factor that into your prep time. If you have trouble finding them at your store, you can substitute the more common white chickpeas instead.

2 tablespoons neutral cooking oil

1 teaspoon cumin seeds

1 teaspoon fennel seeds

1 large onion, finely chopped

1 tablespoon finely minced garlic

1 tablespoon finely minced ginger

2 tablespoons tomato paste

1 tablespoon ground coriander

½ teaspoon ground red chili

½ teaspoon Garam Masala (page 110)

1. Select Sauté mode, adjust the heat to high, and put the oil, cumin seeds, and fennel seeds in the Instant Pot.

2. Once the cumin and fennel seeds start to sizzle, add the onion, garlic, and ginger and cook for 3 to 4 minutes, until the onion begins to brown. Keep stirring occasionally to avoid burning.

3. Add the tomato paste, coriander, red chili, garam masala, amchur powder, and turmeric and season with salt. Mix well.

4. Slowly add the tomatoes and cook for 3 to 4 minutes, until they start to pulp and blend in with the spices.

5. Add the brown chickpeas and water and stir well to combine.

6. Turn off Sauté mode, lock the lid, and close the steam valve. Press Manual and set the timer for 30 minutes on high pressure.

½ teaspoon
   amchur powder
¼ teaspoon ground
   turmeric
Salt
2 medium tomatoes,
   finely chopped
2 cups dried brown
   chickpeas, soaked for
   2 hours in hot water
3 cups water
Fresh cilantro leaves,
   finely chopped,
   for garnish
Freshly squeezed lemon
   juice, for garnish

7. When the timer goes off, let the pressure release naturally for 10 to 12 minutes, then quick release any remaining pressure. Carefully remove the lid.
8. Garnish with cilantro and lemon juice and serve warm.

SUBSTITUTION TIP: If using canned white chickpeas, set the timer for 20 minutes on high pressure.

Per serving: Calories: 427; Total fat: 12g; Saturated fat: 1g; Sodium: 32mg; Carbohydrates: 64g; Sugar: 14g; Fiber: 18g; Protein: 20g; Calcium: 117mg

CHANA SAAG (CHICKPEAS AND SPINACH)

GLUTEN-FREE, NUT-FREE, SOY-FREE

Prep time: 10 minutes **Sauté time:** 8 minutes **Pressure build:** 8 to 10 minutes
Pressure cook: 30 minutes **Pressure release:** Natural, 10 to 12 minutes
Total time: 1 hour, 10 minutes **Serves 4**

This recipe is a family favorite and one of my comfort meals on cold winter nights.
I love to serve it with a side of warm naan and some cool Cucumber Raita (page 107)
or Beetroot Raita (page 106).

2 tablespoons neutral
  cooking oil
1 large onion, finely
  chopped
1 tablespoon finely
  minced garlic
1 tablespoon finely
  minced ginger
2 tablespoons
  tomato paste
1 tablespoon ground
  coriander
½ teaspoon ground
  red chili
½ teaspoon Garam
  Masala (page 110)
¼ teaspoon ground
  turmeric
Salt
2 medium tomatoes,
  finely chopped
4 cups finely chopped
  fresh spinach
3 cups water
2 (15-ounce) cans
  chickpeas, drained
  and rinsed (if using
  dried, soak 1½ cups for
  2 hours in hot water)

1. Select Sauté mode, and adjust the heat to high.
   Put the oil, onion, garlic, and ginger in the Instant
   Pot, and cook for 3 to 4 minutes, until the onion
   begins to brown. Keep stirring occasionally to
   avoid burning.

2. Add the tomato paste, coriander, red chili, garam
   masala, and turmeric and season with salt. Mix well.

3. Slowly add the tomatoes and cook for 3 to 4 minutes,
   until they start to pulp and blend in with the spices.

4. Add the spinach, water, and chickpeas and stir well
   to combine.

5. Turn off Sauté mode, lock the lid, and close the
   steam valve. Press Manual and set the timer for
   20 minutes on high pressure for canned chickpeas or
   30 minutes on high pressure for dried chickpeas.

6. When the timer goes off, let the pressure release
   naturally for 10 to 12 minutes, then quick release any
   remaining pressure. Carefully remove the lid.

7. Serve warm.

Per serving: Calories: 297; Total fat: 11g; Saturated fat: 1g;
Sodium: 317mg; Carbohydrates: 40g; Sugar: 10g; Fiber: 11g;
Protein: 12g; Calcium: 119mg

ZUCCHINI CHANA DAL

GLUTEN-FREE, NUT-FREE, SOY-FREE

Prep time: 10 minutes **Sauté time:** 5 minutes **Pressure build:** 8 to 10 minutes
Pressure cook: 6 minutes **Pressure release:** Natural, 8 to 10 minutes
Total time: 41 minutes **Serves 4**

This is a common recipe found in most parts of Northern India. It is quick and simple to cook, and the addition of zucchini to the dal brings a whole new depth of flavor along with making it a highly nutritious meal.

2 tablespoons neutral cooking oil

1 teaspoon cumin seeds

1 teaspoon fennel seeds

1 medium onion, finely chopped

1 tablespoon finely minced ginger

½ teaspoon ground red chili

½ teaspoon ground coriander

¼ teaspoon ground turmeric

¼ teaspoon amchur powder

Salt

1 medium tomato, finely chopped

2 medium zucchini, roughly chopped

2 cups dried chana dal lentils, rinsed and drained

2 cups water

Fresh cilantro leaves, finely chopped, for garnish

1. Select Sauté mode, adjust the heat to high, and put the oil, cumin seeds, and fennel seeds in the Instant Pot.

2. Once the cumin and fennel seeds start to sizzle, add the onion and ginger and cook for 1 to 2 minutes, until the onion begins to brown. Keep stirring occasionally to avoid burning.

3. Add the red chili, coriander, turmeric, and amchur powder and season with salt. Mix well.

4. Slowly add the tomato and cook for 2 to 3 minutes, until it starts to pulp and blend in with the spices.

5. Add the zucchini, lentils, and water and stir well to combine.

6. Turn off Sauté mode, lock the lid, and close the steam valve. Press Manual and set the timer for 6 minutes on high pressure.

7. When the timer goes off, let the pressure release naturally for 8 to 10 minutes, then quick release any remaining pressure. Carefully remove the lid.

8. Garnish with cilantro and serve warm.

Per serving: Calories: 402; Total fat: 11g; Saturated fat: 1g; Sodium: 12mg; Carbohydrates: 64g; Sugar: 7g; Fiber: 24g; Protein: 16g; Calcium: 198mg

ALU LOBIA (BLACK-EYED PEAS AND POTATO CURRY)

GLUTEN-FREE, NUT-FREE, SOY-FREE

Prep time: 10 minutes **Sauté time:** 8 minutes **Pressure build:** 8 to 10 minutes
Pressure cook: 20 minutes **Pressure release:** Natural, 10 to 12 minutes
Total time: 1 hour **Serves 4**

This simple dish of black-eyed peas and potatoes cooked together in a mild curry is an absolute comfort food. Pair it with a side of Perfect Basmati Rice (page 42) and salad for a complete, well-balanced meal.

2 tablespoons neutral cooking oil

1 teaspoon cumin seeds

1 large onion, finely chopped

1 tablespoon finely minced garlic

1 tablespoon finely minced ginger

1 tablespoon ground coriander

½ teaspoon ground red chili

¼ teaspoon ground turmeric

¼ teaspoon Garam Masala (page 110)

Salt

2 medium tomatoes, finely chopped

3 cups water

2 medium potatoes, quartered

2 cups canned black-eyed peas, drained and rinsed (if using dried, soak for 2 hours in hot water)

Fresh cilantro leaves, finely chopped, for garnish

1. Select Sauté mode, adjust the heat to high, and put the oil and cumin seeds in the Instant Pot.

2. Once the cumin seeds start to sizzle, add the onion, garlic, and ginger and cook for 3 to 4 minutes, until the onion begins to brown. Keep stirring occasionally to avoid burning.

3. Add the coriander, red chili, turmeric, and garam masala and season with salt. Mix well.

4. Slowly add the tomatoes and cook for 3 to 4 minutes, until they start to pulp and blend in with the spices.

5. Add the water, potatoes, and black-eyed peas and stir well to combine.

6. Turn off Sauté mode, lock the lid, and close the steam valve. Press Manual and set the timer for 20 minutes on high pressure for canned black-eyed peas or 25 minutes for dried black-eyed peas.

7. When the timer goes off, let the pressure release naturally for 10 to 12 minutes, then quick release any remaining pressure. Carefully remove the lid.

8. Garnish with cilantro and serve warm.

Per serving: Calories: 262; Total fat: 8g; Saturated fat: 1g; Sodium: 49mg; Carbohydrates: 41g; Sugar: 6g; Fiber: 8g; Protein: 9g; Calcium: 56mg

CHATPATA URAD DAL (TANGY LENTILS)

GLUTEN-FREE, NUT-FREE, SOY-FREE

Prep time: 10 minutes **Sauté time:** 4 minutes **Pressure build:** 8 to 10 minutes
Pressure cook: 8 minutes **Pressure release:** Natural, 8 to 10 minutes
Total time: 42 minutes **Serves 4**

This recipe is a wonderful change from traditional lentil dishes. Serve it with a mild pulao, such as Peas Pulao (page 43), Jeera Rice (page 44), and a fresh salad or Cucumber Raita (page 107) on the side.

2 tablespoons neutral
   cooking oil
1 teaspoon cumin seeds
1 large onion, thinly sliced
1 tablespoon finely
   minced ginger
1 teaspoon ground
   coriander
½ teaspoon ground
   red chili
½ teaspoon
   amchur powder
¼ teaspoon ground
   turmeric
Salt
2 cups dried whole white
   urad lentils, rinsed
   and drained
2 cups water
Fresh cilantro leaves,
   finely chopped,
   for garnish
Freshly squeezed lime
   juice for garnish

1. Select Sauté mode, adjust the heat to high, and put the oil and cumin seeds in the Instant Pot.

2. Once the cumin seeds start to sizzle, add the onion and ginger and cook for 1 to 2 minutes, until the onion begins to brown. Keep stirring occasionally to avoid burning.

3. Add the coriander, red chili, amchur powder, and turmeric and season with salt. Mix well.

4. Add the lentils and water and stir well to combine.

5. Turn off Sauté mode, lock the lid, and close the steam valve. Press Manual and set the timer for 8 minutes on high pressure.

6. When the timer goes off, let the pressure release naturally for 8 to 10 minutes, then quick release any remaining pressure. Carefully remove the lid.

7. Garnish with cilantro and a generous squeeze of lime juice and serve warm.

Per serving: Calories: 323; Total fat: 9g; Saturated fat: 1g; Sodium: 3mg; Carbohydrates: 47g; Sugar: 2g; Fiber: 9g; Protein: 19g; Calcium: 45mg

KHATTI-MEETHI DAL (SWEET AND SOUR LENTILS)

GLUTEN-FREE, NUT-FREE, SOY-FREE

Prep time: 10 minutes **Sauté time:** 8 minutes **Pressure build:** 8 to 10 minutes
Pressure cook: 5 minutes **Pressure release:** Natural, 8 to 10 minutes
Total time: 43 minutes **Serves 4**

This quick and simple dish is my version of the classic Gujarati-style dal with a slight sweet and sour flavor. Sugar and lime juice balance well to create this effect.

2 tablespoons neutral
  cooking oil
6 or 7 fresh curry leaves
1 teaspoon cumin seeds
1 teaspoon mustard seeds
1 medium onion, finely
  chopped
1 tablespoon finely
  minced ginger
1 teaspoon ground
  coriander
½ teaspoon ground
  red chili
¼ teaspoon ground
  turmeric
Salt
1 large tomato, finely
  chopped
2 cups dried yellow lentils,
  rinsed and drained
2 cups water
1 tablespoon sugar
2 tablespoons freshly
  squeezed lime juice
Fresh cilantro leaves,
  finely chopped,
  for garnish

1. Select Sauté mode, adjust the heat to high, and put the oil, curry leaves, cumin seeds, and mustard seeds in the Instant Pot.

2. Once the cumin and mustard seeds start to sizzle, add the onion and ginger and cook for 2 to 3 minutes, until the onion begins to brown. Keep stirring occasionally to avoid burning.

3. Add the coriander, red chili, and turmeric and season with salt. Mix well.

4. Slowly add the tomato and cook for 2 to 3 minutes, until it starts to pulp and blend in with the spices.

5. Add the lentils, water, and sugar and stir well to combine.

6. Turn off Sauté mode, lock the lid, and close the steam valve. Press Manual and set the timer for 5 minutes on high pressure.

7. When the timer goes off, let the pressure release naturally for 8 to 10 minutes, then quick release any remaining pressure. Carefully remove the lid.

8. Garnish with lime juice and cilantro and serve warm.

Per serving: Calories: 446; Total fat: 9g; Saturated fat: 1g; Sodium: 15mg; Carbohydrates: 66g; Sugar: 8g; Fiber: 15g; Protein: 27g; Calcium: 90mg

VEGETABLE BIRYANI, page 46

CHAPTER THREE

RICE DISHES

PERFECT BASMATI RICE

GLUTEN-FREE, NUT-FREE, SOY-FREE, SUPER FAST

Prep time: 1 minute **Pressure build:** 8 to 10 minutes **Pressure cook:** 3 minutes
Pressure release: Natural, 10 minutes **Total time:** 24 minutes **Serves 4**

Basmati rice is one of the most popular types of rice that comes from India. The word basmati means "full of flavor" in Hindi, and the slightly nutty grain is true to its word. It is fragrant and best enjoyed when the rice grains are tender yet not sticky. Be sure to rinse the rice thoroughly until the water runs clear to remove excess starch and ensure separate, distinct grains.

2 cups basmati
   rice, rinsed
3 cups water

1. Put the rice and water in the Instant Pot, lock the lid, and close the steam valve. Press Manual and set the timer for 3 minutes on high pressure.

2. When the timer goes off, let the pressure release naturally for 10 minutes, then quick release any remaining pressure. Carefully remove the lid.

3. Carefully fluff the rice with a fork and serve warm.

PREP TIP: Always remember to use a fork while fluffing the rice when it is warm to keep the grains from clumping with one another.

Per serving: Calories: 320; Total fat: 1g; Saturated fat: 0g; Sodium: 0mg; Carbohydrates: 72g; Sugar: 0g; Fiber: 0g; Protein: 6g; Calcium: 0mg

PEAS PULAO

GLUTEN-FREE, NUT-FREE, SOY-FREE

Prep time: 5 minutes **Sauté time:** 4 minutes **Pressure build:** 8 to 10 minutes **Pressure cook:** 3 minutes **Pressure release:** Natural, 10 minutes **Total time:** 32 minutes **Serves 4**

This simple, flavorful dish involves basmati rice cooked with peas and fragrant spices. It's best enjoyed as a side with curries like Rajma (page 16) or Chana Dal Masala (page 22) and Cucumber Raita (page 107).

1 tablespoon neutral cooking oil
1 teaspoon cumin seeds
1 small onion, thinly sliced
2 cups basmati rice, rinsed
1 cup frozen peas, thawed
3 cups water
Salt
Fresh cilantro leaves, finely chopped, for garnish

1. Select Sauté mode, adjust the heat to high, and put the oil and cumin seeds in the Instant Pot.

2. Once the cumin seeds start to sizzle, add the onion and cook for 1 to 2 minutes, until the onion begins to brown. Keep stirring occasionally to avoid burning.

3. Add the rice and peas and give it a quick stir to mix well.

4. Add the water and season with salt. Mix again.

5. Turn off Sauté mode, lock the lid, and close the steam valve. Press Manual and set the timer for 3 minutes on high pressure.

6. When the timer goes off, let the pressure release naturally for 10 minutes, then quick release any remaining pressure. Carefully remove the lid.

7. Garnish with cilantro and serve warm.

VARIATION: Instead of using just peas, you can add a mix of frozen chopped vegetables to the recipe for more flavor and nutrition.

Per serving: Calories: 385; Total fat: 5g; Saturated fat: 1g; Sodium: 38mg; Carbohydrates: 78g; Sugar: 2g; Fiber: 2g; Protein: 8g; Calcium: 16mg

JEERA RICE (CUMIN RICE)

GLUTEN-FREE, NUT-FREE, SOY-FREE

Prep time: 5 minutes **Sauté time:** 3 minutes **Pressure build:** 8 to 10 minutes **Pressure cook:** 3 minutes **Pressure release:** Natural, 10 minutes **Total time:** 31 minutes **Serves 4**

This fragrant basmati rice cooked with toasted cumin pairs perfectly with curries like Matar Paneer (page 61) or Dal Makhani (page 76).

1 tablespoon neutral
  cooking oil
1 teaspoon cumin seeds
2 cups basmati
  rice, rinsed
3 cups water
Salt
Fresh cilantro leaves,
  finely chopped,
  for garnish

1. Select Sauté mode, adjust the heat to high, and put the oil and cumin seeds in the Instant Pot.

2. Once the cumin seeds start to sizzle, add the rice and give it a quick stir to mix well.

3. Add the water and season with salt. Mix again.

4. Turn off Sauté mode, lock the lid, and close the steam valve. Press Manual and set the timer for 3 minutes on high pressure.

5. When the timer goes off, let the pressure release naturally for 10 minutes, then quick release any remaining pressure. Carefully remove the lid.

6. Garnish with cilantro and serve warm.

VARIATION: You can add in a mix of frozen chopped vegetables along with the rice to the recipe to make a quick and easy version of Vegetable Pulao.

Per serving: Calories: 352; Total fat: 5g; Saturated fat: 1g; Sodium: 1mg; Carbohydrates: 72g; Sugar: 0g; Fiber: <1g; Protein: 6g; Calcium: 5mg

TOMATO RICE

GLUTEN-FREE, NUT-FREE, SOY-FREE

Prep time: 5 minutes **Sauté time:** 5 minutes **Pressure build:** 8 to 10 minutes **Pressure cook:** 3 minutes **Pressure release:** Natural, 10 minutes **Total time:** 33 minutes **Serves 4**

Tomato rice is a popular recipe from South India where rice is cooked in a spiced tomato broth. You can pair it with a vegetable dish like Achari Gobi (page 62) or Alu Baingan (page 63) on the side.

1 tablespoon neutral
cooking oil
1 teaspoon mustard seeds
1 medium onion,
thinly sliced
4 or 5 fresh curry leaves
1 or 2 garlic cloves,
thinly sliced
1 teaspoon ground
coriander
½ teaspoon ground
red chili
¼ teaspoon ground
turmeric
1 large tomato, roughly
chopped
2 cups basmati
rice, rinsed
3 cups water
Salt
Fresh cilantro leaves,
finely chopped,
for garnish

1. Select Sauté mode, adjust the heat to high, and put the oil and mustard seeds in the Instant Pot.

2. Once the mustard seeds start to sizzle, add the onion, curry leaves, and garlic and cook for 2 to 3 minutes, until the onion begins to brown. Keep stirring occasionally to avoid burning.

3. Add the coriander, red chili, and turmeric and mix well.

4. Add the tomato and mix well to coat with the spices.

5. Slowly add the rice and mix well.

6. Add the water and season with salt. Mix again.

7. Turn off Sauté mode, lock the lid, and close the steam valve. Press Manual and set the timer for 3 minutes on high pressure.

8. When the timer goes off, let the pressure release naturally for 10 minutes, then quick release any remaining pressure. Carefully remove the lid.

9. Garnish with cilantro and serve warm.

Per serving: Calories: 378; Total fat: 5g; Saturated fat: 1g; Sodium: 4mg; Carbohydrates: 78g; Sugar: 2g; Fiber: 1g; Protein: 7g; Calcium: 45mg

VEGETABLE BIRYANI

GLUTEN-FREE, NUT-FREE, SOY-FREE

Prep time: 10 minutes **Sauté time:** 6 minutes **Pressure build:** 8 to 10 minutes
Pressure cook: 3 minutes **Pressure release:** Natural, 10 minutes
Total time: 39 minutes **Serves 4**

One of the most popular restaurant favorites, vegetable biryani is a rice-based dish traditionally slow cooked with spiced seasonal vegetables. Here the Instant Pot speeds up the process. For vegetables, I use tomato, potatoes, carrots, peas, and corn, but feel free to experiment with other vegetables you like or have on hand.

2 tablespoons neutral
  cooking oil
1 teaspoon cumin seeds
4 or 5 green
  cardamom pods
4 or 5 whole cloves
1 medium onion,
  thinly sliced
1 tablespoon finely
  minced garlic
1 tablespoon finely
  minced ginger
1 tablespoon ground
  coriander
½ teaspoon ground
  red chili
½ teaspoon Garam
  Masala (page 110)
¼ teaspoon ground
  turmeric
8 baby potatoes, halved
1 medium tomato, cut
  into wedges

1. Select Sauté mode, adjust the heat to high, and put the oil, cumin seeds, cardamom pods, and whole cloves in the Instant Pot.

2. Once the cumin seeds start to sizzle, add the onion, garlic, and ginger and cook for 2 to 3 minutes, until the onion begins to brown. Keep stirring occasionally to avoid burning.

3. Add the coriander, red chili, garam masala, and turmeric and mix well.

4. Add the tomato, potatoes, carrots, peas, and corn and mix well to coat with the spices.

5. Slowly add the rice and mix well. Add the water and season with salt. Mix again.

6. Turn off Sauté mode, lock the lid, and close the steam valve. Press Manual and set the timer for 3 minutes on high pressure.

1 cup sliced carrots
½ cup frozen peas, thawed
½ cup frozen
   corn, thawed
2 cups basmati rice, rinsed
3 cups water
Salt
Fresh cilantro leaves,
   finely chopped,
   for garnish
Fresh mint leaves, finely
   chopped, for garnish

7. When the timer goes off, let the pressure release naturally for 10 minutes, then quick release any remaining pressure. Carefully remove the lid.

8. Garnish with cilantro and mint and serve warm.

Per serving: Calories: 518; Total fat: 9g; Saturated fat: 1g; Sodium: 139mg; Carbohydrates: 99g; Sugar: 5g; Fiber: 3g; Protein: 11g; Calcium: 45mg

LEMON RICE

GLUTEN-FREE, SOY-FREE

Prep time: 5 minutes **Sauté time:** 5 minutes **Pressure build:** 8 to 10 minutes **Pressure cook:** 3 minutes **Pressure release:** Natural, 10 minutes **Total time:** 33 minutes **Serves 4**

Another South Indian dish, lemon rice is served mostly during lunch. The lemon adds a slight tang to the dish and the peanuts offer a nice crunch. If you don't have peanuts, swap them for cashews. This rice goes great with Sambhar (page 20) and Bharwan Baingan (page 68).

1 tablespoon neutral
   cooking oil
1 teaspoon mustard seeds
1 medium onion,
   thinly sliced
4 or 5 fresh curry leaves
¼ cup raw peanuts
1 teaspoon ground
   coriander
½ teaspoon ground
   red chili
¼ teaspoon ground
   turmeric
2 cups basmati
   rice, rinsed
3 cups water
Salt
2 tablespoons freshly
   squeezed lemon juice
Fresh cilantro leaves,
   finely chopped,
   for garnish

1. Select Sauté mode, adjust the heat to high, and put the oil and mustard seeds in the Instant Pot.

2. Once the mustard seeds start to sizzle, add the onion and curry leaves and cook for 2 to 3 minutes, until the onion begins to brown. Keep stirring occasionally to avoid burning.

3. Add the peanuts, coriander, red chili, and turmeric and mix well.

4. Slowly add the rice and mix well. Add the water and season with salt. Mix again.

5. Turn off Sauté mode, lock the lid, and close the steam valve. Press Manual and set the timer for 3 minutes on high pressure.

6. When the timer goes off, let the pressure release naturally for 10 minutes, then quick release any remaining pressure. Carefully remove the lid.

7. Garnish with lemon juice and cilantro and serve warm.

Per serving: Calories: 420; Total fat: 9g; Saturated fat: 1g; Sodium: 3mg; Carbohydrates: 78g; Sugar: 2g; Fiber: 1g; Protein: 9g; Calcium: 48mg

KICHDI

GLUTEN-FREE, NUT-FREE, SOY-FREE

Prep time: 5 minutes **Sauté time:** 4 minutes **Pressure build:** 8 to 10 minutes **Pressure cook:** 3 minutes **Pressure release:** Natural, 10 minutes **Total time:** 32 minutes **Serves 4**

Kichdi is a quick and simple comfort dish that's made with mildly spiced rice and dal or lentils. Red lentils are the quickest to cook, but you can also use moong or chana dal. Adding vegetables like carrots, potatoes, peas, or cauliflower is a good way to bulk up the recipe and make it more nutrient dense.

1 tablespoon neutral cooking oil
1 teaspoon cumin seeds
1 small onion, thinly sliced
1 teaspoon finely minced garlic
1 teaspoon finely minced ginger
1 medium tomato, finely chopped
1 teaspoon ground coriander
½ teaspoon ground red chili
¼ teaspoon ground turmeric
1 cup dried red lentils, rinsed
2 cups basmati rice, rinsed
4 cups water
Salt
Fresh cilantro leaves, finely chopped, for garnish

1. Select Sauté mode, adjust the heat to high, and put the oil and cumin seeds in the Instant Pot.

2. Once the cumin seeds start to sizzle, add the onion, garlic, and ginger and cook for 1 to 2 minutes, until the onion begins to brown. Keep stirring occasionally to avoid burning.

3. Add the tomato, coriander, red chili, and turmeric and mix well.

4. Slowly add the lentils and rice and mix well. Add the water and season with salt. Mix again.

5. Turn off Sauté mode, lock the lid, and close the steam valve. Press Manual and set the timer for 3 minutes on high pressure.

6. When the timer goes off, let the pressure release naturally for 10 minutes, then quick release any remaining pressure. Carefully remove the lid.

7. Garnish with cilantro and serve warm.

Per serving: Calories: 539; Total fat: 6g; Saturated fat: 1g; Sodium: 9mg; Carbohydrates: 104g; Sugar: 3g; Fiber: 8g; Protein: 20g; Calcium: 35mg

CHANA PULAO

GLUTEN-FREE, NUT-FREE, SOY-FREE

Prep time: 5 minutes **Sauté time:** 4 minutes **Pressure build:** 8 to 10 minutes **Pressure cook:**
3 minutes **Pressure release:** Natural, 10 minutes **Total time:** 32 minutes **Serves 4**

A flavorful rice-based dish cooked with chickpeas and seasoned with fragrant whole spices, this recipe is perfect when you're short on time and want a quick, comforting meal. Pair it with Cucumber Raita (page 107) or Mint Chutney (page 104) on the side as an accompaniment.

1 tablespoon neutral
cooking oil
1 teaspoon cumin seeds
1 small onion, thinly sliced
1 teaspoon finely
minced garlic
1 teaspoon finely
minced ginger
1 cup canned
chickpeas, rinsed
1 teaspoon ground
coriander
½ teaspoon ground
red chili
¼ teaspoon ground
turmeric
¼ teaspoon Garam
Masala (page 110)
2 cups basmati
rice, rinsed
3 cups water
Salt
Fresh cilantro leaves,
finely chopped,
for garnish

1. Select Sauté mode, adjust the heat to high, and put the oil and cumin seeds in the Instant Pot.

2. Once the cumin seeds start to sizzle, add the onion, garlic, and ginger and cook for 1 to 2 minutes, until the onion begins to brown. Keep stirring occasionally to avoid burning.

3. Add the chickpeas, coriander, red chili, turmeric, and garam masala and mix well.

4. Slowly add the rice and mix well. Add the water and season with salt. Mix again.

5. Turn off Sauté mode, lock the lid, and close the steam valve. Press Manual and set the timer for 3 minutes on high pressure.

6. When the timer goes off, let the pressure release naturally for 10 minutes, then quick release any remaining pressure. Carefully remove the lid.

7. Garnish with cilantro and serve warm.

Per serving: Calories: 416; Total fat: 6g; Saturated fat: 1g;
Sodium: 83mg; Carbohydrates: 83g; Sugar: 2g; Fiber: 3g;
Protein: 9g; Calcium: 29mg

COCONUT RICE

GLUTEN-FREE, SOY-FREE

Prep time: 5 minutes **Sauté time:** 3 minutes **Pressure build:** 8 to 10 minutes **Pressure cook:** 3 minutes **Pressure release:** Natural, 10 minutes **Total time:** 31 minutes **Serves 4**

This basmati rice is cooked in coconut milk and flavored with curry leaves and spices. This recipe pairs perfectly with Beetroot Raita (page 106) or Tomato Chutney (page 103) on the side.

1 tablespoon neutral
   cooking oil
1 teaspoon mustard seeds
1 medium onion,
   thinly sliced
4 or 5 fresh curry leaves
2 cups basmati
   rice, rinsed
2 cups water
1 cup full-fat coconut milk
Salt
Fresh cilantro leaves,
   finely chopped,
   for garnish

1. Select Sauté mode, adjust the heat to high, and put the oil and mustard seeds in the Instant Pot.

2. Once the mustard seeds start to sizzle, add the onion and curry leaves and cook for 2 to 3 minutes, until the onion begins to brown. Keep stirring occasionally to avoid burning.

3. Slowly add the rice and mix well. Add the water and coconut milk and season with salt. Mix again.

4. Turn off Sauté mode, lock the lid, and close the steam valve. Press Manual and set the timer for 3 minutes on high pressure.

5. When the timer goes off, let the pressure release naturally for 10 minutes, then quick release any remaining pressure. Carefully remove the lid.

6. Garnish with cilantro and serve warm.

PREP TIP: Make sure to give your coconut milk a good mix before adding it into the pot. This will ensure that the fat is evenly distributed and blends in well with the rice.

Per serving: Calories: 469; Total fat: 15g; Saturated fat: 10g; Sodium: 7mg; Carbohydrates: 78g; Sugar: 3g; Fiber: 1g; Protein: 8g; Calcium: 39mg

RAJMA PULAO

GLUTEN-FREE, NUT-FREE, SOY-FREE

Prep time: 5 minutes **Sauté time:** 4 minutes **Pressure build:** 8 to 10 minutes **Pressure cook:** 3 minutes **Pressure release:** Natural, 10 minutes **Total time:** 32 minutes **Serves 4**

Rajma pulao is a flavorful rice-based dish cooked with red kidney beans and seasoned with fragrant whole spices. Serve it with vegetable dishes like Kaddu ki Sabzi (page 72) or Kadhai Mushroom (page 71) with Cucumber Raita (page 107).

1 tablespoon neutral cooking oil
1 teaspoon cumin seeds
1 small onion, thinly sliced
1 teaspoon finely minced garlic
1 teaspoon finely minced ginger
1 cup canned red kidney beans, drained and rinsed
1 medium tomato, finely chopped
1 teaspoon ground coriander
½ teaspoon ground red chili
¼ teaspoon ground turmeric
2 cups basmati rice, rinsed
3 cups water
Salt
Fresh cilantro leaves, finely chopped, for garnish

1. Select Sauté mode, adjust the heat to high, and put the oil and cumin seeds in the Instant Pot.

2. Once the cumin seeds start to sizzle, add the onion, garlic, and ginger and cook for 1 to 2 minutes, until the onion begins to brown. Keep stirring occasionally to avoid burning.

3. Add the kidney beans, tomato, coriander, red chili, and turmeric and mix well.

4. Slowly add the rice and mix well. Add the water and season with salt. Mix again.

5. Turn off Sauté mode, lock the lid, and close the steam valve. Press Manual and set the timer for 3 minutes on high pressure.

6. When the timer goes off, let the pressure release naturally for 10 minutes, then quick release any remaining pressure. Carefully remove the lid.

7. Garnish with cilantro and serve warm.

Per serving: Calories: 418; Total fat: 5g; Saturated fat: 1g; Sodium: 86mg; Carbohydrates: 84g; Sugar: 3g; Fiber: 3g; Protein: 10g; Calcium: 37mg

PALAK RICE

GLUTEN-FREE, NUT-FREE, SOY-FREE

Prep time: 5 minutes **Sauté time:** 4 minutes **Pressure build:** 8 to 10 minutes **Pressure cook:** 3 minutes **Pressure release:** Natural, 10 minutes **Total time:** 32 minutes **Serves 4**

Also known as green rice due to its vibrant color, this popular recipe consists of basmati rice cooked with finely chopped spinach. You can also use frozen spinach instead to make this even easier.

1 tablespoon neutral cooking oil
1 teaspoon cumin seeds
1 small onion, thinly sliced
1 teaspoon finely minced garlic
2 cups finely chopped fresh spinach
1 medium tomato, finely chopped
1 teaspoon ground coriander
½ teaspoon ground red chili
2 cups basmati rice, rinsed
3 cups water
Salt

1. Select Sauté mode, adjust the heat to high, and put the oil and cumin seeds in the Instant Pot.

2. Once the cumin seeds start to sizzle, add the onion and garlic and cook for 1 to 2 minutes, until the onion begins to brown. Keep stirring occasionally to avoid burning.

3. Add the spinach, tomato, coriander, and red chili and mix well.

4. Slowly add the rice and mix well. Add the water and season with salt. Mix again.

5. Turn off Sauté mode, lock the lid, and close the steam valve. Press Manual and set the timer for 3 minutes on high pressure.

6. When the timer goes off, let the pressure release naturally for 10 minutes, then quick release any remaining pressure. Carefully remove the lid.

7. Serve warm.

Per serving: Calories: 370; Total fat: 5g; Saturated fat: 1g; Sodium: 15mg; Carbohydrates: 76g; Sugar: 2g; Fiber: 1g; Protein: 7g; Calcium: 29mg

KASHMIRI PULAO

GLUTEN-FREE, SOY-FREE

Prep time: 5 minutes **Sauté time:** 3 minutes **Pressure build:** 8 to 10 minutes **Pressure cook:** 3 minutes **Pressure release:** Natural, 10 minutes **Total time:** 31 minutes **Serves 4**

A traditional pulao from the northernmost part of India, this dish is flavored with dried fruit and nuts. While this pulao uses a combination of cashews, almonds, and raisins, you can mix and match any other dried fruits and nuts you have on hand to make it your own.

1 tablespoon neutral
   cooking oil
1 teaspoon cumin seeds
2 cups basmati
   rice, rinsed
¼ cup roughly chopped
   cashews
¼ cup roughly chopped
   almonds
¼ cup raisins
3 cups water
Salt
Fresh cilantro leaves,
   finely chopped,
   for garnish

1. Select Sauté mode, adjust the heat to high, and put the oil and cumin seeds in the Instant Pot.

2. Once the cumin seeds start to sizzle, add the rice, cashews, almonds, and raisins and mix well.

3. Add the water and season with salt. Mix again.

4. Turn off Sauté mode, lock the lid, and close the steam valve. Press Manual and set the timer for 3 minutes on high pressure.

5. When the timer goes off, let the pressure release naturally for 10 minutes, then quick release any remaining pressure. Carefully remove the lid.

6. Garnish with cilantro and serve warm.

Per serving: Calories: 471; Total fat: 12g; Saturated fat: 1g; Sodium: 4mg; Carbohydrates: 84g; Sugar: 7g; Fiber: 2g; Protein: 10g; Calcium: 35mg

TEHRI

GLUTEN-FREE, NUT-FREE, SOY-FREE

Prep time: 5 minutes **Sauté time:** 4 minutes **Pressure build:** 8 to 10 minutes **Pressure cook:** 3 minutes **Pressure release:** Natural, 10 minutes **Total time:** 32 minutes **Serves 4**

Tehri is a typical one-pot homestyle recipe made with rice and potatoes and is usually served as a quick lunch with a side of raita. Try this with either Cucumber Raita (page 107) or Beetroot Raita (page 106). You can also add carrots and cauliflower to bulk up the recipe even more.

1 tablespoon neutral
  cooking oil
1 teaspoon cumin seeds
1 small onion, thinly sliced
1 teaspoon finely
  minced garlic
1 teaspoon finely
  minced ginger
2 medium potatoes,
  quartered
½ cup frozen
  peas, thawed
1 teaspoon ground
  coriander
½ teaspoon ground
  red chili
¼ teaspoon ground
  turmeric
2 cups basmati
  rice, rinsed
3 cups water
Salt
Fresh cilantro leaves,
  finely chopped,
  for garnish

1. Select Sauté mode, adjust the heat to high, and put the oil and cumin seeds in the Instant Pot.

2. Once the cumin seeds start to sizzle, add the onion, garlic, and ginger and cook for 1 to 2 minutes, until the onion begins to brown. Keep stirring occasionally to avoid burning.

3. Add the potatoes, peas, coriander, red chili, and turmeric and mix well.

4. Slowly add the rice and mix well. Add the water and season with salt. Mix again.

5. Turn off Sauté mode, lock the lid, and close the steam valve. Press Manual and set the timer for 3 minutes on high pressure.

6. When the timer goes off, let the pressure release naturally for 10 minutes, then quick release any remaining pressure. Carefully remove the lid.

7. Garnish with cilantro and serve warm.

Per serving: Calories: 449; Total fat: 5g; Saturated fat: 1g; Sodium: 37mg; Carbohydrates: 94g; Sugar: 3g; Fiber: 4g; Protein: 9g; Calcium: 25mg

MASALA PULAO

GLUTEN-FREE, NUT-FREE, SOY-FREE

Prep time: 5 minutes **Sauté time:** 4 minutes **Pressure build:** 8 to 10 minutes **Pressure cook:** 3 minutes **Pressure release:** Natural, 10 minutes **Total time:** 32 minutes **Serves 4**

A spicy dish of basmati rice cooked with sautéed onions and tomatoes, this pulao is great eaten on its own with Cucumber Raita (page 107) or paired with Khatti-Meethi Dal (page 38) on the side.

1 tablespoon neutral cooking oil
1 teaspoon cumin seeds
1 small onion, thinly sliced
1 teaspoon finely minced garlic
1 teaspoon finely minced ginger
1 large tomato, roughly chopped
1 teaspoon ground coriander
½ teaspoon ground red chili
¼ teaspoon ground turmeric
¼ teaspoon Garam Masala (page 110)
2 cups basmati rice, rinsed
3 cups water
Salt
Fresh cilantro leaves, finely chopped, for garnish

1. Select Sauté mode, adjust the heat to high, and put the oil and cumin seeds in the Instant Pot.

2. Once the cumin seeds start to sizzle, add the onion, garlic, and ginger and cook for 1 to 2 minutes, until the onion begins to brown. Keep stirring occasionally to avoid burning.

3. Add the tomato, coriander, red chili, turmeric, and garam masala and mix well.

4. Slowly add the rice and mix well. Add the water and season with salt. Mix again.

5. Turn off Sauté mode, lock the lid, and close the steam valve. Press Manual and set the timer for 3 minutes on high pressure.

6. When the timer goes off, let the pressure release naturally for 10 minutes, then quick release any remaining pressure. Carefully remove the lid.

7. Garnish with cilantro and serve warm.

Per serving: Calories: 371; Total fat: 5g; Saturated fat: 1g; Sodium: 4mg; Carbohydrates: 76g; Sugar: 2g; Fiber: 1g; Protein: 7g; Calcium: 16mg

POTATO MINT PULAO

GLUTEN-FREE, NUT-FREE, SOY-FREE

Prep time: 5 minutes **Sauté time:** 4 minutes **Pressure build:** 8 to 10 minutes **Pressure cook:** 3 minutes **Pressure release:** Natural, 10 minutes **Total time:** 32 minutes **Serves 4**

This is a quick pulao made with chopped potatoes and simply seasoned with spices and fresh mint. Serve this with Dal Tadka (page 21) and Saag Paneer (page 82).

1 tablespoon neutral
  cooking oil
1 teaspoon cumin seeds
1 small onion, thinly sliced
2 medium potatoes, cut
  into 1-inch pieces
1 teaspoon ground
  coriander
½ teaspoon ground
  red chili
¼ teaspoon ground
  turmeric
2 cups basmati
  rice, rinsed
3 cups water
Salt
Fresh mint leaves, finely
  chopped, for garnish

1. Select Sauté mode, adjust the heat to high, and put the oil and cumin seeds in the Instant Pot.

2. Once the cumin seeds start to sizzle, add the onion and cook for 1 to 2 minutes, until the onion begins to brown. Keep stirring occasionally to avoid burning.

3. Add the potatoes, coriander, red chili, and turmeric and mix well.

4. Slowly add the rice and mix well. Add the water and season with salt. Mix again.

5. Turn off Sauté mode, lock the lid, and close the steam valve. Press Manual and set the timer for 3 minutes on high pressure.

6. When the timer goes off, let the pressure release naturally for 10 minutes, then quick release any remaining pressure. Carefully remove the lid.

7. Garnish with mint and serve warm.

Per serving: Calories: 434; Total fat: 5g; Saturated fat: 1g; Sodium: 19mg; Carbohydrates: 91g; Sugar: 2g; Fiber: 3g; Protein: 8g; Calcium: 21mg

ALU MATAR, page 60

CHAPTER FOUR

CURRIES

ALU MATAR (POTATO AND PEA CURRY)

GLUTEN-FREE, NUT-FREE, SOY-FREE

Prep time: 10 minutes **Sauté time:** 8 minutes **Pressure build:** 8 to 10 minutes
Pressure cook: 2 minutes **Pressure release:** Natural, 10 to 12 minutes
Total time: 42 minutes **Serves 4**

This quick and light potato and pea curry is cooked in a mildly spiced tomato-based gravy. Pair this with Jeera Rice (page 44) and a vegetable dish like Achari Gobi (page 62) or Achari Paneer Tikka (page 80).

2 tablespoons neutral cooking oil
1 teaspoon cumin seeds
1 large onion, finely chopped
1 tablespoon finely minced garlic
1 tablespoon ground coriander
½ teaspoon ground red chili
¼ teaspoon ground turmeric
Salt
2 medium tomatoes, finely chopped
4 medium potatoes, diced into bite-size cubes
2 cups frozen peas, thawed
2 cups water
Fresh cilantro leaves, finely chopped, for garnish

1. Select Sauté mode, adjust the heat to high, and put the oil and cumin seeds in the Instant Pot.

2. Once the cumin seeds start to sizzle, add the onion and garlic and cook for 3 to 4 minutes, until the onion begins to brown. Keep stirring occasionally to avoid burning.

3. Add the coriander, red chili, and turmeric and season with salt. Mix well.

4. Slowly add the tomatoes and cook for 3 to 4 minutes, until they start to pulp and blend in with the spices.

5. Add the potatoes, peas, and water and stir well to combine.

6. Turn off Sauté mode, lock the lid, and close the steam valve. Press Manual and set the timer for 2 minutes on high pressure.

7. When the timer goes off, let the pressure release naturally for 10 to 12 minutes, then quick release any remaining pressure. Carefully remove the lid.

8. Garnish with cilantro and serve warm.

Per serving: Calories: 293; Total fat: 8g; Saturated fat: 1g; Sodium: 113g; Carbohydrates: 50g; Sugar: 9g; Fiber: 10g; Protein: 8g; Calcium: 60mg

MATAR PANEER
(PEA AND TOFU CURRY)

GLUTEN-FREE, NUT-FREE

Prep time: 10 minutes **Sauté time:** 8 minutes **Pressure build:** 8 to 10 minutes
Pressure cook: 2 minutes **Pressure release:** Natural, 10 to 12 minutes
Total time: 42 minutes **Serves 4**

This paneer and pea curry is a classic dish made vegan by using tofu instead of paneer. Extra-firm tofu is very similar to paneer in texture and can easily absorb the flavors of the spices.

2 tablespoons neutral
  cooking oil
1 teaspoon cumin seeds
1 large onion, finely
  chopped
1 tablespoon finely
  minced garlic
1 tablespoon finely
  minced ginger
2 tablespoons
  tomato paste
1 tablespoon
  ground coriander
½ teaspoon ground
  red chili
½ teaspoon
  ground cumin
Salt
2 medium tomatoes,
  finely chopped
10½ ounces extra-firm
  tofu, cut into
  bite-size cubes
2 cups frozen
  peas, thawed
2 cups water
Fresh cilantro leaves,
  finely chopped,
  for garnish

1. Select Sauté mode, adjust the heat to high, and put the oil and cumin seeds in the Instant Pot.

2. Once the cumin seeds start to sizzle, add the onion, garlic, and ginger and cook for 3 to 4 minutes, until the onion begins to brown. Keep stirring occasionally to avoid burning.

3. Add the tomato paste, coriander, red chili, and cumin and season with salt. Mix well.

4. Slowly add the tomatoes and cook for 3 to 4 minutes, until they start to pulp and blend in with the spices.

5. Add the tofu, peas, and water and stir well to combine.

6. Turn off Sauté mode, lock the lid, and close the steam valve. Press Manual and set the timer for 2 minutes on high pressure.

7. When the timer goes off, let the pressure release naturally for 10 to 12 minutes, then quick release any remaining pressure. Carefully remove the lid.

8. Garnish with cilantro and serve warm.

Per serving: Calories: 235; Total fat: 12g; Saturated fat: 2g; Sodium: 89mg; Carbohydrates: 21g; Sugar: 8g; Fiber: 6g; Protein: 13g; Calcium: 159mg

ACHARI GOBI (SPICED CAULIFLOWER)

GLUTEN-FREE, NUT-FREE, SOY-FREE

Prep time: 10 minutes **Sauté time:** 5 minutes **Pressure build:** 8 to 10 minutes
Pressure cook: 2 minutes **Pressure release:** Natural, 10 to 12 minutes
Total time: 39 minutes **Serves 4**

This mildly spiced, quick, and simple stir-fry with cauliflower florets is a popular dish served in many restaurants. It pairs perfectly well with rice or rotis and a lentil like Dal Tadka (page 21) on the side.

2 tablespoons neutral
  cooking oil
1 tablespoon Paanch
  Phoron (page 112)
1 large onion,
  finely chopped
1 tablespoon finely
  minced garlic
1 tablespoon finely
  minced ginger
2 tablespoons
  tomato paste
1 tablespoon
  ground coriander
½ teaspoon ground
  red chili
½ teaspoon
  amchur powder
Salt
1 cauliflower head, cut into
  bite-size florets
½ cup water
Fresh cilantro leaves,
  finely chopped,
  for garnish

1. Select Sauté mode, adjust the heat to high, and put the oil and paanch phoron in the Instant Pot.

2. Once the paanch phoron starts to sizzle, add the onion, garlic, and ginger and cook for 3 to 4 minutes, until the onion begins to brown. Keep stirring occasionally to avoid burning.

3. Add the tomato paste, coriander, red chili, and amchur powder and season with salt. Mix well.

4. Slowly add the cauliflower and water and mix well with the spices.

5. Turn off Sauté mode, lock the lid, and close the steam valve. Press Manual and set the timer for 2 minutes on high pressure.

6. When the timer goes off, let the pressure release naturally for 10 to 12 minutes, then quick release any remaining pressure. Carefully remove the lid.

7. Garnish with cilantro and serve warm.

INGREDIENT TIP: You can also use frozen cauliflower florets if you don't have any fresh.

Per serving: Calories: 138; Total fat: 8g; Saturated fat: 1g; Sodium: 53mg; Carbohydrates: 15g; Sugar: 6g; Fiber: 4g; Protein: 4g; Calcium: 58mg

ALU BAINGAN (EGGPLANT AND POTATO CURRY)

GLUTEN-FREE, NUT-FREE, SOY-FREE

Prep time: 10 minutes **Sauté time:** 6 minutes **Pressure build:** 8 to 10 minutes
Pressure cook: 2 minutes **Pressure release:** Natural, 10 to 12 minutes
Total time: 40 minutes **Serves 4**

This is a classic North Indian recipe made by sautéing eggplants and potatoes with tomatoes and a blend of spices. Serve it with some fresh warm naan and Chana Dal Masala (page 22).

2 tablespoons neutral
  cooking oil
1 teaspoon cumin seeds
1 large onion,
  finely chopped
1 tablespoon finely
  minced garlic
1 tablespoon finely
  minced ginger
1 tablespoon tomato paste
1 tablespoon
  ground coriander
¼ teaspoon ground
  turmeric
¼ teaspoon ground
  red chili
¼ teaspoon Garam
  Masala (page 110)
Salt
2 medium potatoes, cut
  into bite-size pieces
3 Japanese or Chinese
  eggplants, cut into
  1-inch pieces
2 medium tomatoes, cut
  into wedges
1 cup water
Fresh cilantro, finely
  chopped, for garnish

1. Select Sauté mode, adjust the heat to high, and put the oil and cumin seeds in the Instant Pot.

2. Once the cumin seeds start to sizzle, add the onion, garlic, and ginger and cook for 3 to 4 minutes, until the onion begins to brown. Keep stirring occasionally to avoid burning.

3. Add the tomato paste, coriander, turmeric, red chili, and garam masala and season with salt. Mix well.

4. Add the potatoes and eggplants and cook for 1 to 2 minutes to mix well with the spices.

5. Add the tomatoes and water and stir well to combine.

6. Turn off Sauté mode, lock the lid, and close the steam valve. Press Manual and set the timer for 2 minutes on high pressure.

7. When the timer goes off, let the pressure release naturally for 10 to 12 minutes, then quick release any remaining pressure. Carefully remove the lid.

8. Garnish with cilantro and serve warm.

Per serving: Calories: 268; Total fat: 7g; Saturated fat: 1g; Sodium: 26mg; Carbohydrates: 44g; Sugar: 16g; Fiber: 12g; Protein: 7g; Calcium: 37mg

GAJAR GOBI MATAR (CARROTS, CAULIFLOWER, AND PEAS)

GLUTEN-FREE, NUT-FREE, SOY-FREE

Prep time: 10 minutes **Sauté time:** 5 minutes **Pressure build:** 8 to 10 minutes
Pressure cook: 2 minutes **Pressure release:** Natural, 10 to 12 minutes
Total time: 39 minutes **Serves 4**

Literally translating to "carrots, cauliflower, peas," this dish is a classic winter specialty made in many Indian homes and served with a side of fresh rotis and some dal. You can also use a mix of frozen peas and carrots if you're short on time.

2 tablespoons neutral
　　cooking oil
1 teaspoon cumin seeds
1 medium onion, finely
　　chopped
1 tablespoon tomato paste
1 tablespoon ground
　　coriander
¼ teaspoon ground
　　turmeric
¼ teaspoon ground
　　red chili
¼ teaspoon
　　amchur powder
Salt
4 cups cauliflower florets
2 cups chopped carrots
2 cups frozen
　　peas, thawed
1 cup water
Fresh cilantro, finely
　　chopped, for garnish

1. Select Sauté mode, adjust the heat to high, and put the oil and cumin seeds in the Instant Pot.

2. Once the cumin seeds start to sizzle, add the onion and cook for 2 to 3 minutes, until the onion begins to brown. Keep stirring occasionally to avoid burning.

3. Add the tomato paste, coriander, turmeric, red chili, and amchur powder and season with salt. Mix well.

4. Add the cauliflower, carrots, and peas and cook for 1 to 2 minutes to mix well with the spices. Add the water and stir well to combine.

5. Turn off Sauté mode, lock the lid, and close the steam valve. Press Manual and set the timer for 2 minutes on high pressure.

6. When the timer goes off, let the pressure release naturally for 10 to 12 minutes, then quick release any remaining pressure. Carefully remove the lid.

7. Garnish with cilantro and serve warm.

Per serving: Calories: 184; Total fat: 8g; Saturated fat: 1g; Sodium: 154mg; Carbohydrates: 25g; Sugar: 10g; Fiber: 8g; Protein: 7g; Calcium: 78mg

BAINGAN BHARTA (SPICED EGGPLANT MASH)

GLUTEN-FREE, NUT-FREE, SOY-FREE

Prep time: 10 minutes **Sauté time:** 8 minutes **Pressure build:** 8 to 10 minutes
Pressure cook: 3 minutes **Pressure release:** Quick **Total time:** 31 minutes **Serves 4**

This is a classic Punjabi favorite traditionally made by roasting whole eggplants and sautéing them in a blend of tomatoes and spices. This dish is best enjoyed with rotis and Dal Tadka (page 21) on the side.

2 tablespoons neutral cooking oil
1 teaspoon cumin seeds
1 large onion, finely chopped
1 tablespoon finely minced ginger
½ teaspoon ground red chili
¼ teaspoon Garam Masala (page 110)
Salt
2 medium tomatoes, finely chopped
2 large eggplants, cut into bite-size cubes
½ cup water
Fresh cilantro leaves, finely chopped, for garnish

1. Select Sauté mode, adjust the heat to high, and put the oil and cumin seeds in the Instant Pot.

2. Once the cumin seeds start to sizzle, add the onion and ginger and cook for 3 to 4 minutes, until the onion begins to brown. Keep stirring occasionally to avoid burning.

3. Add the red chili and garam masala and season with salt. Mix well.

4. Slowly stir in the tomatoes and cook for 3 to 4 minutes, until they start to pulp and blend in with the spices.

5. Add the eggplants and water and stir well to combine.

6. Turn off Sauté mode, lock the lid, and close the steam valve. Press Manual and set the timer for 3 minutes on high pressure.

7. When the timer goes off, quick release the pressure. Carefully open the lid and slowly mash the eggplant. Give it a quick stir to mix everything well.

8. Garnish with cilantro and serve warm.

Per serving: Calories: 178; Total fat: 8g; Saturated fat: 1g; Sodium: 13mg; Carbohydrates: 27g; Sugar: 15g; Fiber: 12g; Protein: 5g; Calcium: 51mg

MUSHROOM MATAR (MUSHROOM AND PEA CURRY)

GLUTEN-FREE, NUT-FREE, SOY-FREE

Prep time: 10 minutes **Sauté time:** 8 minutes **Pressure build:** 8 to 10 minutes
Pressure cook: 2 minutes **Pressure release:** Natural, 10 to 12 minutes
Total time: 42 minutes **Serves 4**

Fresh mushrooms and peas are cooked in a rich spice blend with sautéed onions and tomatoes in mushroom matar. I use cremini mushrooms here, but feel free to use other mushrooms you might have on hand, such as button or shiitake.

2 tablespoons neutral
cooking oil
1 large onion, finely
chopped
1 tablespoon finely
minced garlic
1 tablespoon finely
minced ginger
1 tablespoon
tomato paste
1 tablespoon ground
coriander
½ teaspoon ground
red chili
¼ teaspoon ground
turmeric
¼ teaspoon Garam
Masala (page 110)
Salt
2 medium tomatoes,
finely chopped
18 to 20 cremini
mushrooms, quartered
2 cups frozen
peas, thawed
1 cup water
Fresh cilantro leaves,
finely chopped,
for garnish

1. Select Sauté mode, adjust the heat to high, and put the oil in the Instant Pot.

2. Once the oil starts to warm up, add the onion, garlic, and ginger and cook for 3 to 4 minutes, until the onion begins to brown. Keep stirring occasionally to avoid burning.

3. Add the tomato paste, coriander, red chili, turmeric, and garam masala and season with salt. Mix well.

4. Slowly add the tomatoes and cook for 3 to 4 minutes, until they start to pulp and blend in with the spices.

5. Add the mushrooms, peas, and water and stir well to combine.

6. Turn off Sauté mode, lock the lid, and close the steam valve. Press Manual and set the timer for 2 minutes on high pressure.

7. When the timer goes off, let the pressure release naturally for 10 to 12 minutes, then quick release any remaining pressure. Carefully remove the lid.

8. Garnish with cilantro and serve warm.

Per serving: Calories: 171; Total fat: 8g; Saturated fat: 1g; Sodium: 85mg; Carbohydrates: 20g; Sugar: 9g; Fiber: 6g; Protein: 8g; Calcium: 41mg

VEGETABLE KORMA

GLUTEN-FREE, SOY-FREE

Prep time: 10 minutes **Sauté time:** 6 minutes **Pressure build:** 8 to 10 minutes
Pressure cook: 3 minutes **Pressure release:** Natural, 10 to 12 minutes
Total time: 41 minutes **Serves 4**

Vegetable korma is a decadent mixed vegetable curry simmered in a fragrantly spiced coconut-based sauce. Serve it with Perfect Basmati Rice (page 42) and Achari Paneer Tikka (page 80).

2 tablespoons neutral cooking oil
1 cinnamon stick
3 or 4 whole green cardamom pods
1 large onion, finely chopped
1 tablespoon finely minced garlic
1 tablespoon finely minced ginger
1 tablespoon ground coriander
½ teaspoon ground red chili
¼ teaspoon ground turmeric
Salt
2 cups chopped carrots
2 cups chopped potatoes
2 cups chopped cauliflower florets
2 cups chopped green beans
2 cups frozen peas, thawed
1 cup full-fat coconut milk
½ cup water
Fresh cilantro leaves, finely chopped, for garnish

1. Select Sauté mode, adjust the heat to high, and put the oil, cinnamon stick, and cardamom pods in the Instant Pot.

2. Once the oil starts to warm up, add the onion, garlic, and ginger and cook for 3 to 4 minutes, until the onion begins to brown. Keep stirring occasionally to avoid burning.

3. Add the coriander, red chili, and turmeric and season with salt. Mix well.

4. Add the carrots, potatoes, cauliflower, green beans, and peas and cook for 1 to 2 minutes, until they blend in with the spices.

5. Add the coconut milk and water and stir well to combine.

6. Turn off Sauté mode, lock the lid, and close the steam valve. Press Manual and set the timer for 3 minutes on high pressure.

7. When the timer goes off, let the pressure release naturally for 10 to 12 minutes, then quick release any remaining pressure. Carefully remove the lid.

8. Garnish with cilantro and serve warm.

Per serving: Calories: 346; Total fat: 18g; Saturated fat: 10g; Sodium: 156mg; Carbohydrates: 42g; Sugar: 14g; Fiber: 10g; Protein: 9g; Calcium: 92mg

BHARWAN BAINGAN (STUFFED EGGPLANTS)

GLUTEN-FREE, NUT-FREE, SOY-FREE

Prep time: 10 minutes **Sauté time:** 1 minute **Pressure build:** 8 to 10 minutes **Pressure cook:** 3 minutes **Pressure release:** Natural, 10 to 12 minutes **Total time:** 36 minutes **Serves 4**

These baby eggplants stuffed with a mix of spices and cooked until tender and flavorful are a favorite of mine. Serve this with a flavored rice dish like Peas Pulao (page 43) and Kali Dal (page 23).

2 tablespoons ground coriander
½ teaspoon ground red chili
½ teaspoon Garam Masala (page 110)
½ teaspoon garlic powder
¼ teaspoon ground turmeric
Salt
6 to 8 small round baby eggplants
2 tablespoons neutral cooking oil
¼ cup water
Fresh cilantro leaves, finely chopped, for garnish

1. In a small bowl, mix the coriander, red chili, garam masala, garlic powder, and turmeric and season with salt. Set aside.

2. With a knife, start at the round end and make two cuts in a cross halfway through each eggplant, being careful not to cut them all the way through. You want to be able to fill them with the spice mix while preserving their shape.

3. Carefully stuff each eggplant with the spice mix and set aside.

4. Select Sauté mode, adjust the heat to high, and put the oil in the Instant Pot.

5. Once the oil starts to warm up, carefully place the stuffed eggplants in the Instant Pot. Sprinkle any leftover spice mix on top. Give it a quick stir and add the water. Mix again.

6. Turn off Sauté mode, lock the lid, and close the steam valve. Press Manual and set the timer for 3 minutes on high pressure.

7. When the timer goes off, let the pressure release naturally for 10 to 12 minutes, then quick release any remaining pressure. Carefully remove the lid.

8. Garnish with cilantro and serve warm.

Per serving: Calories: 103; Total fat: 7g; Saturated fat: 1g; Sodium: 3mg; Carbohydrates: 9g; Sugar: 3g; Fiber: 5g; Protein: 2g; Calcium: 43mg

BHINDI DO PIAZA
(OKRA WITH ONIONS)

GLUTEN-FREE, NUT-FREE, SOY-FREE, SUPER FAST

Prep time: 10 minutes **Sauté time:** 6 minutes **Pressure build:** 8 to 10 minutes
Pressure cook: 3 minutes **Pressure release:** Quick **Total time:** 29 minutes **Serves 4**

This tangy stir-fried okra with onions and a mix of spices is a fragrant, delicious dish. This recipe is best paired with a lentil like Mixed Dal (page 26) or Khatti-Meethi Dal (page 38) and rice or rotis on the side. Add in a side salad or chutney to complete the meal.

2 tablespoons neutral cooking oil
1 teaspoon cumin seeds
1 large onion, thinly sliced
1 tablespoon ground coriander
½ teaspoon ground red chili
¼ teaspoon ground turmeric
¼ teaspoon amchur powder
Salt
25 to 30 okra, cut into 1-inch pieces
1 medium tomato, finely chopped
¼ cup water

1. Select Sauté mode, adjust the heat to high, and put the oil and cumin seeds in the Instant Pot.

2. Once the cumin seeds start to sizzle, add the onion and cook for 1 to 2 minutes, until the onion begins to brown. Keep stirring occasionally to avoid burning.

3. Add the coriander, red chili, turmeric, and amchur powder and season with salt to taste. Mix well.

4. Slowly stir in the okra and tomato and cook for 3 to 4 minutes, until they mix in well with the spices.

5. Add the water and stir well to combine.

6. Turn off Sauté mode, lock the lid, and close the steam valve. Press Manual and set the timer for 3 minutes on high pressure.

7. When the timer goes off, quick release the pressure.

8. Serve warm.

INGREDIENT TIP: When chopping the okra, make sure that you wipe them dry first to prevent them from getting slimy.

Per serving: Calories: 111; Total fat: 7g; Saturated fat: 1g; Sodium: 10mg; Carbohydrates: 11g; Sugar: 4g; Fiber: 4g; Protein: 2g; Calcium: 84mg

ALU BHAJI (POTATO CURRY)

GLUTEN-FREE, NUT-FREE, SOY-FREE

Prep time: 10 minutes **Sauté time:** 8 minutes **Pressure build:** 8 to 10 minutes
Pressure cook: 3 minutes **Pressure release:** Quick **Total time:** 31 minutes **Serves 4**

This traditional potato curry is usually served with puris as a weekend brunch meal. You can also serve it with naan and Instant Chile Achaar (page 105) for a quick lunch or dinner.

2 tablespoons neutral cooking oil
1 teaspoon cumin seeds
1 large onion, finely chopped
1 tablespoon finely minced garlic
1 tablespoon finely minced ginger
2 tablespoons tomato paste
1 tablespoon ground coriander
½ teaspoon ground red chili
¼ teaspoon ground turmeric
¼ teaspoon Garam Masala (page 110)
Salt
2 medium tomatoes, finely chopped
4 medium potatoes, cut into bite-size cubes
2 cups water
Fresh cilantro leaves, finely chopped, for garnish

1. Select Sauté mode, adjust the heat to high, and put the oil and cumin seeds in the Instant Pot.

2. Once the cumin seeds start to sizzle, add the onion, garlic, and ginger and cook for 3 to 4 minutes, until the onion begins to brown. Keep stirring occasionally to avoid burning.

3. Add the tomato paste, coriander, red chili, turmeric, and garam masala and season with salt. Mix well.

4. Slowly add the tomatoes and cook for 3 to 4 minutes, until they start to pulp and blend in with the spices.

5. Add the potatoes and water and stir well to combine.

6. Turn off Sauté mode, lock the lid, and close the steam valve. Press Manual and set the timer for 3 minutes on high pressure.

7. When the timer goes off, quick release the pressure.

8. Carefully open the lid and roughly mash the potatoes to give the curry a chunky texture. Give it a quick stir to mix everything well.

9. Garnish with cilantro and serve warm.

Per serving: Calories: 252; Total fat: 8g; Saturated fat: 1g; Sodium: 46mg; Carbohydrates: 43g; Sugar: 7g; Fiber: 7g; Protein: 5g; Calcium: 48mg

KADHAI MUSHROOM (MUSHROOMS AND PEPPERS)

GLUTEN-FREE, NUT-FREE, SOY-FREE

Prep time: 10 minutes **Sauté time:** 6 minutes **Pressure build:** 8 to 10 minutes
Pressure cook: 2 minutes **Pressure release:** Natural, 10 minutes
Total time: 38 minutes **Serves 4**

Fresh cremini mushrooms are stir-fried with a mix of peppers and onions and added to a tangy tomato-based sauce. "Kadhai" refers to the Indian version of the Chinese wok, the cooking vessel traditionally used to make this dish. Here the Instant Pot does all the heavy lifting, and the recipe comes together in a snap.

2 tablespoons neutral cooking oil
1 teaspoon cumin seeds
1 large onion, thinly sliced
1 tablespoon finely minced garlic
1 tablespoon finely minced ginger
1 tablespoon tomato paste
1 tablespoon ground coriander
½ teaspoon ground red chili
¼ teaspoon ground turmeric
Salt
18 to 20 cremini mushrooms, quartered
1 large tomato, thinly sliced
1 green bell pepper, thinly sliced
¼ cup water
Fresh cilantro leaves, finely chopped, for garnish

1. Select Sauté mode, adjust the heat to high, and put the oil and cumin seeds in the Instant Pot.

2. Once the cumin seeds start to sizzle, add the onion, garlic, and ginger and cook for 1 to 2 minutes, until the onion begins to brown. Keep stirring occasionally to avoid burning.

3. Add the tomato paste, coriander, red chili, and turmeric and season with salt. Mix well.

4. Add the mushrooms and cook for 3 to 4 minutes, until they start to lightly brown along the edges and blend in with the spices.

5. Slowly stir in the tomato and bell pepper, add the water, and mix well to combine.

6. Turn off Sauté mode, lock the lid, and close the steam valve. Press Manual and set the timer for 2 minutes on high pressure.

7. When the timer goes off, let the pressure release naturally for 10 minutes, then quick release any remaining pressure. Carefully remove the lid.

8. Garnish with cilantro and serve warm.

Per serving: Calories: 124; Total fat: 8g; Saturated fat: 1g; Sodium: 14mg; Carbohydrates: 12g; Sugar: 6g; Fiber: 3g; Protein: 4g; Calcium: 30mg

KADDU KI SABZI (SPICED BUTTERNUT SQUASH)

GLUTEN-FREE, NUT-FREE, SOY-FREE

Prep time: 10 minutes **Sauté time:** 4 minutes **Pressure build:** 8 to 10 minutes
Pressure cook: 3 minutes **Pressure release:** Natural, 10 minutes
Total time: 37 minutes **Serves 4**

This is a sweet and sour Punjabi-style pumpkin curry dish, made here with butternut squash. The amchur powder gives it a tanginess, but if you don't have it on hand, use freshly squeezed lime juice instead. Serve it with fresh parathas.

2 tablespoons neutral cooking oil

4 cups fresh cubed butternut squash (or frozen and thawed)

1 tablespoon finely minced ginger

1 tablespoon ground coriander

½ teaspoon ground red chili

¼ teaspoon ground turmeric

¼ teaspoon amchur powder

Salt

1 cup water

1. Select Sauté mode, adjust the heat to high, and put the oil in the Instant Pot.

2. Once the oil starts to warm up, add the butternut squash and ginger and cook for 3 to 4 minutes, stirring occasionally to avoid burning.

3. Add the coriander, red chili, turmeric, and amchur powder and season with salt. Mix well.

4. Add the water and stir well to combine.

5. Turn off Sauté mode, lock the lid, and close the steam valve. Press Manual and set the timer for 3 minutes on high pressure.

6. When the timer goes off, let the pressure release naturally for 10 minutes, then quick release any remaining pressure. Carefully remove the lid.

7. Roughly mash the butternut squash to give the curry a chunky texture. Give it a quick stir to mix everything well.

8. Serve warm.

VARIATION: You can use sweet potatoes instead of butternut squash in this recipe.

Per serving: Calories: 150; Total fat: 7g; Saturated fat: 1g; Sodium: 9mg; Carbohydrates: 23g; Sugar: 4g; Fiber: 7g; Protein: 2g; Calcium: 90mg

CORN MASALA CURRY

GLUTEN-FREE, NUT-FREE, SOY-FREE

Prep time: 10 minutes **Sauté time:** 8 minutes **Pressure build:** 8 to 10 minutes
Pressure cook: 2 minutes **Pressure release:** Natural, 10 minutes
Total time: 40 minutes **Serves 4**

This is a quick and simple dish to make. A spicy tomato curry makes up the base, and frozen corn kernels add a touch of sweetness and color. Try this with fresh corn when it is readily available during the summer months.

2 tablespoons neutral cooking oil

1 teaspoon cumin seeds

1 large onion, finely chopped

1 tablespoon finely minced garlic

1 tablespoon finely minced ginger

2 tablespoons tomato paste

1 tablespoon ground coriander

½ teaspoon ground red chili

½ teaspoon ground cumin

¼ teaspoon Garam Masala (page 110)

Salt

2 medium tomatoes, finely chopped

4 cups frozen corn kernels, thawed

2 cups water

Fresh cilantro leaves, finely chopped, for garnish

1. Select Sauté mode, adjust the heat to high, and put the oil and cumin seeds in the Instant Pot.

2. Once the cumin seeds start to sizzle, add the onion, garlic, and ginger and cook for 3 to 4 minutes, until the onion begins to brown. Keep stirring occasionally to avoid burning.

3. Add the tomato paste, coriander, red chili, cumin, and garam masala and season with salt. Mix well.

4. Slowly add the tomatoes and cook for 3 to 4 minutes, until they start to pulp and blend in with the spices.

5. Add the corn and water and stir well to combine.

6. Turn off Sauté mode, lock the lid, and close the steam valve. Press Manual and set the timer for 2 minutes on high pressure.

7. When the timer goes off, let the pressure release naturally for 10 minutes, then quick release any remaining pressure. Carefully remove the lid.

8. Garnish with cilantro and serve warm.

Per serving: Calories: 225; Total fat: 8g; Saturated fat: 1g; Sodium: 16mg; Carbohydrates: 38g; Sugar: 8g; Fiber: 5g; Protein: 6g; Calcium: 37mg

GOBI TIKKA MASALA, page 81

CHAPTER FIVE

FAVORITES REIMAGINED

DAL MAKHANI
(CREAMY BLACK LENTILS)

GLUTEN-FREE, NUT-FREE, SOY-FREE

Prep time: 10 minutes **Sauté time:** 8 minutes **Pressure build:** 8 to 10 minutes
Pressure cook: 25 minutes **Pressure release:** Natural, 10 to 12 minutes
Total time: 1 hour, 5 minutes **Serves 4**

Dal makhani, popular in North Indian cuisine, is a restaurant favorite made from black lentils (urad dal) simmered down to a smooth buttery consistency. Traditionally, it's made with dairy, but plant-based milks work just as well to create a creamy dal.

2 tablespoons neutral
   cooking oil
1 medium onion, finely
   chopped
1 tablespoon finely
   minced garlic
1 tablespoon finely
   minced ginger
1 tablespoon tomato paste
1 teaspoon ground
   coriander
½ teaspoon ground
   red chili
Salt
2 medium tomatoes,
   finely chopped
2 cups water, plus more
   as needed
1 cup dried whole black
   lentils, rinsed
¼ cup canned red
   kidney beans, drained
   and rinsed
2 tablespoons plant-based
   milk of choice
Fresh cilantro leaves,
   finely chopped,
   for garnish

1. Select Sauté mode, adjust the heat to high, and put the oil in the Instant Pot.

2. Once the oil starts to warm up, add the onion, garlic, and ginger and cook for 3 to 4 minutes, until the onion begins to brown. Keep stirring occasionally to avoid burning.

3. Add the tomato paste, coriander, and red chili and season with salt. Mix well.

4. Slowly add the tomatoes and cook for 3 to 4 minutes, until they start to pulp and blend in with the spices.

5. Add the water, lentils, and kidney beans and stir well to combine.

6. Turn off Sauté mode, lock the lid, and close the steam valve. Press Manual and set the timer for 25 minutes on high pressure.

7. When the timer goes off, let the pressure release naturally for 10 to 12 minutes, then quick release any remaining pressure.

8. Carefully open the lid and set the Instant Pot back to Sauté mode.

9. Slowly stir in the plant-based milk and let it come to a boil. You can also add more water at this point depending on the consistency you prefer. Give it a quick stir to mix everything well.

10. Garnish with cilantro and serve warm.

Per serving: Calories: 252; Total fat: 8g; Saturated fat: 1g; Sodium: 36mg; Carbohydrates: 34g; Sugar: 5g; Fiber: 12g; Protein: 14g; Calcium: 56mg

PANEER BURJI (SPICED CRUMBLED TOFU)

GLUTEN-FREE, NUT-FREE

Prep time: 10 minutes **Sauté time:** 6 minutes **Pressure build:** 8 to 10 minutes
Pressure cook: 2 minutes **Pressure release:** Natural, 10 to 12 minutes
Total time: 40 minutes **Serves 4**

This is a vegan version of the spicy Indian dish traditionally made with scrambled eggs. We get the same crumbly, scrambled texture here with extra-firm tofu, which picks up the spices nicely. This is best served with toast for a hearty brunch.

2 tablespoons neutral
  cooking oil
1 medium onion,
  thinly sliced
1 tablespoon
  ground coriander
½ teaspoon ground
  red chili
¼ teaspoon ground
  turmeric
Salt
1 large tomato, finely
  chopped
16 ounces extra-firm
  tofu, drained, pressed,
  and grated
½ cup water
Fresh cilantro leaves,
  finely chopped,
  for garnish

1. Select Sauté mode, adjust the heat to high, and put the oil in the Instant Pot.

2. Once the oil starts to warm up, add the onion and cook for 1 to 2 minutes, until the onion begins to brown. Keep stirring occasionally to avoid burning.

3. Add the coriander, red chili, and turmeric and season with salt. Mix well.

4. Slowly add the tomato and cook for 3 to 4 minutes, until it starts to pulp and blend in with the spices.

5. Add the tofu and water and stir well to combine.

6. Turn off Sauté mode, lock the lid, and close the steam valve. Press Manual and set the timer for 2 minutes on high pressure.

7. When the timer goes off, let the pressure release naturally for 10 to 12 minutes, then quick release any remaining pressure. Carefully remove the lid.

8. Garnish with cilantro and serve warm.

INGREDIENT TIP: Make sure you use only extra-firm tofu to get the desired crumbly texture.

Per serving: Calories: 202; Total fat: 13g; Saturated fat: 2g; Sodium: 11mg; Carbohydrates: 9g; Sugar: 2g; Fiber: 2g; Protein: 13g; Calcium: 191mg

KEEMA MATAR (GROUND "MEAT" AND PEAS)

GLUTEN-FREE, NUT-FREE

Prep time: 10 minutes **Sauté time:** 8 minutes **Pressure build:** 8 to 10 minutes
Pressure cook: 5 minutes **Pressure release:** Natural, 10 to 12 minutes
Total time: 45 minutes **Serves 4**

This mouthwatering classic is traditionally made with ground meat and peas. Here we use textured soy protein to get a meatier texture, and cook it with a blend of spices and tomatoes. This dish is usually served with parathas, flaky, layered flatbreads that are a staple in many Indian homes.

2 tablespoons neutral cooking oil

1 large onion, finely chopped

1 tablespoon finely minced garlic

1 tablespoon finely minced ginger

1 tablespoon ground coriander

½ teaspoon ground red chili

½ teaspoon Garam Masala (page 110)

¼ teaspoon ground turmeric

Salt

1 large tomato, finely chopped

2 cups textured soy protein

1 cup frozen peas, thawed

1 cup water

Fresh cilantro leaves, finely chopped, for garnish

1. Select Sauté mode, adjust the heat to high, and put the oil in the Instant Pot.

2. Once the oil starts to warm up, add the onion, garlic, and ginger and cook for 3 to 4 minutes, until the onion begins to brown. Keep stirring occasionally to avoid burning.

3. Add the coriander, red chili, garam masala, and turmeric and season with salt. Mix well.

4. Slowly add the tomato and cook for 3 to 4 minutes, until it starts to pulp and blend in with the spices.

5. Add the soy protein and peas and cook for 1 to 2 minutes, mixing everything well.

6. Add the water and stir well to combine.

7. Turn off Sauté mode, lock the lid, and close the steam valve. Press Manual and set the timer for 5 minutes on high pressure.

8. When the timer goes off, let the pressure release naturally for 10 to 12 minutes, then quick release any remaining pressure. Carefully remove the lid.

9. Garnish with cilantro and serve warm.

Per serving: Calories: 319; Total fat: 11g; Saturated fat: 1g; Sodium: 41mg; Carbohydrates: 24g; Sugar: 8g; Fiber: 10g; Protein: 20g; Calcium: 28mg

ACHARI PANEER TIKKA

GLUTEN-FREE, NUT-FREE, SUPER FAST

Prep time: 10 minutes **Sauté time:** 3 minutes **Pressure build:** 8 to 10 minutes
Pressure cook: 2 minutes **Pressure release:** Quick **Total time:** 25 minutes **Serves 4**

This is a vegan version of one of the most popular Indian restaurant appetizers, made with cubes of extra-firm tofu. The tofu here is a great substitute for paneer since it is very similar in texture and won't overpower the recipe with its own flavor.

2 tablespoons neutral
   cooking oil
1 teaspoon Paanch
   Phoron (page 112)
10½ ounces extra-firm
   tofu, cut into
   bite-size cubes
½ cup vegan yogurt
   of choice
2 tablespoons
   tomato paste
1 tablespoon Tandoori
   Masala (page 111)
1 tablespoon ground
   coriander
Salt
¼ cup water
Fresh cilantro leaves,
   finely chopped,
   for garnish

1. Select Sauté mode, adjust the heat to high, and put the oil and paanch phoron in the Instant Pot.

2. Once the paanch phoron starts to sizzle, add the tofu and cook for 1 to 2 minutes, until it begins to brown along the edges. Keep stirring occasionally to avoid burning.

3. Add the yogurt, tomato paste, tandoori masala, and coriander and season with salt. Mix well to coat the tofu completely.

4. Add the water and stir well to combine.

5. Turn off Sauté mode, lock the lid, and close the steam valve. Press Manual and set the timer for 2 minutes on high pressure.

6. When the timer goes off, quick release the pressure. Carefully remove the lid.

7. Garnish with cilantro and serve warm.

Per serving: Calories: 175; Total fat: 13g; Saturated fat: 2g; Sodium: 107mg; Carbohydrates: 6g; Sugar: 1g; Fiber: 2g; Protein: 9g; Calcium: 133mg

GOBI TIKKA MASALA (SPICED CAULIFLOWER CURRY)

GLUTEN-FREE, NUT-FREE, SOY-FREE

Prep time: 10 minutes **Sauté time:** 8 minutes **Pressure build:** 8 to 10 minutes
Pressure cook: 4 minutes **Pressure release:** Natural, 10 to 12 minutes
Total time: 44 minutes **Serves 4**

This is a vegan variation of the restaurant favorite chicken tikka masala, made with fresh cauliflower florets. I love using cauliflower here since it keeps its shape after cooking and absorbs the flavor of the spices really well.

2 tablespoons neutral
  cooking oil
1 large onion, finely
  chopped
1 tablespoon finely
  minced garlic
1 tablespoon finely
  minced ginger
½ cup vegan yogurt
  of choice
2 tablespoons
  tomato paste
1 tablespoon Tandoori
  Masala (page 111)
1 tablespoon ground
  coriander
Salt
1 cauliflower head, cut into
  bite-size florets
1 cup water
Fresh cilantro leaves,
  finely chopped,
  for garnish

1. Select Sauté mode, adjust the heat to high, and put the oil in the Instant Pot.

2. Once the oil starts to warm up, add the onion, garlic, and ginger and cook for 3 to 4 minutes, until the onion begins to brown. Keep stirring occasionally to avoid burning.

3. Add the yogurt, tomato paste, tandoori masala, and coriander and season with salt. Mix well.

4. Slowly add the cauliflower and cook for 3 to 4 minutes, stirring occasionally so that the florets are well coated with the spices and yogurt.

5. Add the water and stir well to combine.

6. Turn off Sauté mode, lock the lid, and close the steam valve. Press Manual and set the timer for 4 minutes on high pressure.

7. When the timer goes off, let the pressure release naturally for 10 to 12 minutes, then quick release any remaining pressure. Carefully remove the lid.

8. Garnish with cilantro and serve warm.

Per serving: Calories: 152; Total fat: 10g; Saturated fat: 1g; Sodium: 148mg; Carbohydrates: 15g; Sugar: 6g; Fiber: 4g; Protein: 5g; Calcium: 57mg

SAAG PANEER (SPINACH AND TOFU)

GLUTEN-FREE, NUT-FREE

Prep time: 10 minutes **Sauté time:** 8 minutes **Pressure build:** 8 to 10 minutes
Pressure cook: 4 minutes **Pressure release:** Natural, 10 to 12 minutes
Total time: 44 minutes **Serves 4**

Saag paneer is a classic vegetarian Indian dish. As the name implies, it's made with paneer, a non-melting soft cheese sometimes referred to as Indian cottage cheese. This recipe is made vegan by using lightly sautéed cubes of tofu in a rich blended spinach sauce.

2½ cups frozen
  spinach, thawed
1 cup water, divided
2 tablespoons neutral
  cooking oil
1 medium onion, finely
  chopped
1 tablespoon finely
  minced garlic
1 tablespoon finely
  minced ginger
1 tablespoon tomato paste
1 teaspoon ground
  coriander
½ teaspoon ground
  red chili
¼ teaspoon Garam
  Masala (page 110)
Salt
1 large tomato,
  finely chopped
10½ ounces extra-firm
  tofu, drained, pressed,
  and cut into
  bite-size cubes
Fresh cilantro leaves,
  finely chopped,
  for garnish

1. In a blender or food processor, blend the spinach with ½ cup of water into a smooth puree.

2. Select Sauté mode, adjust the heat to high, and put the oil in the Instant Pot.

3. Once the oil starts to warm up, add the onion, garlic, and ginger and cook for 3 to 4 minutes, until the onion begins to brown. Keep stirring occasionally to avoid burning.

4. Add the tomato paste, coriander, red chili, and garam masala and season with salt. Mix well.

5. Add the tomato and cook for 3 to 4 minutes, until it starts to pulp and blend in with the spices.

6. Slowly add the spinach puree and remaining ½ cup of water and stir well to combine. Add the tofu and mix again.

7. Turn off Sauté mode, lock the lid, and close the steam valve. Press Manual and set the timer for 4 minutes on high pressure.

8. When the timer goes off, let the pressure release naturally for 10 to 12 minutes, then quick release any remaining pressure. Carefully remove the lid.

9. Garnish with cilantro and serve warm.

Per serving: Calories: 199; Total fat: 12g; Saturated fat: 1g; Sodium: 84mg; Carbohydrates: 13g; Sugar: 4g; Fiber: 5g; Protein: 13g; Calcium: 258mg

KEEMA PULAO
(GROUND "MEAT" AND RICE)

GLUTEN-FREE, NUT-FREE

Prep time: 10 minutes **Sauté time:** 5 minutes **Pressure build:** 8 to 10 minutes
Pressure cook: 3 minutes **Pressure release:** Natural, 10 to 12 minutes
Total time: 40 minutes **Serves 4**

This is a quick and simple pulao. Traditionally, it's layered with ground meat and peas and seasoned with fragrant whole spices. This version includes soy protein for a similar texture to the original dish.

2 tablespoons neutral cooking oil
1 teaspoon cumin seeds
1 cinnamon stick
3 or 4 whole green cardamom pods
1 medium onion, thinly sliced
1 teaspoon ground coriander
½ teaspoon ground red chili
Salt
1 large tomato, finely chopped
4 cups water
2 cups basmati rice, rinsed
1 cup textured soy protein
Fresh cilantro leaves, finely chopped, for garnish

1. Select Sauté mode, adjust the heat to high, and put the oil, cumin seeds, cinnamon stick, and cardamom pods in the Instant Pot.

2. Once the cumin seeds start to sizzle, add the onion and cook for 1 to 2 minutes, until the onion begins to brown. Keep stirring occasionally to avoid burning.

3. Add the coriander and red chili and season with salt. Mix well.

4. Add the tomato and cook for 2 to 3 minutes, until it starts to pulp and blend in with the spices.

5. Add the water, rice, and soy protein and stir well to combine.

6. Turn off Sauté mode, lock the lid, and close the steam valve. Press Manual and set the timer for 3 minutes on high pressure.

7. When the timer goes off, let the pressure release naturally for 10 to 12 minutes, then quick release any remaining pressure. Carefully remove the lid.

8. Garnish with cilantro and serve warm.

Per serving: Calories: 503; Total fat: 10g; Saturated fat: 1g; Sodium: 5mg; Carbohydrates: 83g; Sugar: 4g; Fiber: 5g; Protein: 16g; Calcium: 20mg

PANEER BIRYANI

GLUTEN-FREE, NUT-FREE

Prep time: 10 minutes **Sauté time:** 4 minutes **Pressure build:** 8 to 10 minutes
Pressure cook: 3 minutes **Pressure release:** Natural, 10 to 12 minutes
Total time: 39 minutes **Serves 4**

Biryani is a rice-based dish, traditionally made by layering rice and marinated meat or vegetables, and then letting them slow cook until tender and aromatic. This vegan version of the restaurant classic is made with marinated tofu.

2 tablespoons neutral
  cooking oil
1 teaspoon cumin seeds
1 medium onion,
  thinly sliced
10½ ounces extra-firm
  tofu, cut into
  bite-size cubes
1 teaspoon Tandoori
  Masala (page 111)
1 teaspoon ground
  coriander
Salt
3 cups water
2 cups basmati
  rice, rinsed
1 large tomato,
  thinly sliced
Fresh cilantro leaves,
  finely chopped,
  for garnish

1. Select Sauté mode, adjust the heat to high, and put the oil and cumin seeds in the Instant Pot.

2. Once the cumin seeds start to sizzle, add the onion and cook for 1 to 2 minutes, until the onion begins to brown. Keep stirring occasionally to avoid burning.

3. Add the tofu, tandoori masala, and coriander and season with salt. Cook for 1 to 2 minutes to coat the tofu with the spices.

4. Add the water, rice, and tomato, and stir well to combine.

5. Turn off Sauté mode, lock the lid, and close the steam valve. Press Manual and set the timer for 3 minutes on high pressure.

6. When the timer goes off, let the pressure release naturally for 10 to 12 minutes, then quick release any remaining pressure. Carefully remove the lid.

7. Garnish with cilantro and serve warm.

INGREDIENT TIP: Make sure you use only extra-firm tofu to avoid the tofu breaking and blending in with the rice.

Per serving: Calories: 481; Total fat: 12g; Saturated fat: 1g; Sodium: 41mg; Carbohydrates: 80g; Sugar: 2g; Fiber: 2g; Protein: 15g; Calcium: 131mg

METHI MALAI ("CHICKEN" CURRY)

GLUTEN-FREE

Prep time: 10 minutes **Sauté time:** 6 minutes **Pressure build:** 8 to 10 minutes
Pressure cook: 3 minutes **Pressure release:** Natural, 10 to 12 minutes
Total time: 41 minutes **Serves 4**

Adapted from a very popular chicken recipe, this dish uses extra-firm tofu to up the
protein. If you don't want to use tofu, you can use chickpeas and potatoes in its place.
It also uses kasoori methi, or fenugreek leaves, to add flavor and is simmered in a
coconut-based curry for a nice, creamy texture.

2 tablespoons neutral
 cooking oil
1 large onion, finely
 chopped
1 tablespoon finely
 minced garlic
1 tablespoon finely
 minced ginger
2 tablespoons
 kasoori methi
1 tablespoon ground
 coriander
½ teaspoon ground
 red chili
¼ teaspoon Garam
 Masala (page 110)
Salt
10½ ounces extra-firm
 tofu, cut into
 bite-size cubes
1 cup full-fat coconut milk
½ cup water
Fresh cilantro leaves,
 finely chopped,
 for garnish

1. Select Sauté mode, adjust the heat to high, and put
   the oil in the Instant Pot.

2. Once the oil starts to warm up, add the onion, garlic
   and ginger and cook for 3 to 4 minutes, until the
   onion begins to brown. Keep stirring occasionally to
   avoid burning.

3. Add the kasoori methi, coriander, red chili, and
   garam masala and season with salt. Mix well.

4. Add the tofu and cook for 1 to 2 minutes, until they
   are well coated with the spices.

5. Add the coconut milk and water and stir well
   to combine.

6. Turn off Sauté mode, lock the lid, and close the
   steam valve. Press Manual and set the timer for
   3 minutes on high pressure.

7. When the timer goes off, let the pressure release
   naturally for 10 to 12 minutes, then quick release any
   remaining pressure. Carefully remove the lid.

8. Garnish with cilantro and serve warm.

Per serving: Calories: 270; Total fat: 22g; Saturated fat: 11g;
Sodium: 15mg; Carbohydrates: 11g; Sugar: 4g; Fiber: 2g;
Protein: 10g; Calcium: 131mg

ALU GOSHT ("MEAT" AND POTATO CURRY)

GLUTEN-FREE, NUT-FREE

Prep time: 10 minutes **Sauté time:** 8 minutes **Pressure build:** 8 to 10 minutes
Pressure cook: 3 minutes **Pressure release:** Natural, 10 to 12 minutes
Total time: 43 minutes **Serves 4**

This is a vegan version of the classic meat and potato curry using textured soy protein. It's a very popular recipe served in many restaurants and is usually made with lamb or beef. The textured soy protein has a similar texture to the original dish and soaks up all the flavor of the curry.

2 tablespoons neutral cooking oil
1 cinnamon stick
1 teaspoon cumin seeds
1 large onion, finely chopped
1 tablespoon finely minced garlic
1 tablespoon finely minced ginger
1 tablespoon ground coriander
½ teaspoon ground red chili
½ teaspoon Garam Masala (page 110)
Salt
2 medium tomatoes, finely chopped
2 medium potatoes, quartered
3 cups textured soy protein
2 cups water
Fresh cilantro leaves, finely chopped, for garnish

1. Select Sauté mode, adjust the heat to high, and put the oil, cinnamon stick, and cumin seeds in the Instant Pot.

2. Once the cumin seeds start to sizzle, add the onion, garlic, and ginger and cook for 3 to 4 minutes, until the onion begins to brown. Keep stirring occasionally to avoid burning.

3. Add the coriander, red chili, and garam masala and season with salt. Mix well.

4. Slowly add the tomatoes and cook for 3 to 4 minutes, until they start to pulp and blend in with the spices.

5. Add the potatoes, soy protein, and water and stir well to combine.

6. Turn off Sauté mode, lock the lid, and close the steam valve. Press Manual and set the timer for 3 minutes on high pressure.

7. When the timer goes off, let the pressure release naturally for 10 to 12 minutes, then quick release any remaining pressure. Carefully remove the lid.

8. Garnish with cilantro and serve warm.

Per serving: Calories: 471; Total fat: 13g; Saturated fat: 1g; Sodium: 24mg; Carbohydrates: 43g; Sugar: 10g; Fiber: 15g; Protein: 29g; Calcium: 36mg

MANGO SABUDANA KHEER, page 90

CHAPTER SIX

DESSERTS

MANGO SABUDANA KHEER (MANGO TAPIOCA PUDDING)

GLUTEN-FREE, SOY-FREE

Prep time: 5 minutes **Pressure build:** 8 to 10 minutes **Pressure cook:** 5 minutes, then 2 minutes
Pressure release: Quick, then Natural for 10 minutes **Total time:** 32 minutes **Serves 6**

This mildly sweet pudding is made with mango, tapioca pearls, and coconut milk. You should be able to find the white tapioca pearls, called sabudana, at any Indian grocery store. Nowadays, they're also easily available at most regular grocery stores—usually in the international aisle.

2 cups water
1 cup sabudana, rinsed
1½ cups full-fat
   coconut milk
½ cup sugar
1 teaspoon ground
   cardamom
2 cups finely chopped
   fresh mango

1. Put the water and sabudana in the Instant Pot. Lock the lid, close the steam valve, and set the timer for 5 minutes on high pressure. When the timer goes off, quick release the pressure.

2. Open the lid carefully and slowly stir in the coconut milk, sugar, and cardamom to mix well.

3. Lock the lid, close the steam valve, and set the timer for 2 minutes on high pressure.

4. When the timer goes off, let the pressure release naturally for about 10 minutes, then quick release any remaining pressure. Carefully remove the lid.

5. Top with the mango right before serving.

VARIATION: This recipe can be served warm or cold depending on your preference. You can also add a bit of chopped nuts and/or toasted coconut flakes with the mango for an added crunch.

Per serving: Calories: 291; Total fat: 11g; Saturated fat: 9g; Sodium: 7mg; Carbohydrates: 50g; Sugar: 27g; Fiber: 2g; Protein: 1g; Calcium: 15mg

SOOJI HALWA (SEMOLINA HALWA)

SOY-FREE

Prep time: 5 minutes **Sauté:** 5 minutes **Pressure build:** 8 to 10 minutes **Pressure cook:** 2 minutes **Pressure release:** Natural, 10 minutes **Total time:** 32 minutes **Serves 6**

Halwa is an Indian pudding, generally creamy in texture and made from a variety of grains, fruits, or vegetables. This is a traditional version of the homestyle pudding and is made using semolina.

¼ cup neutral cooking oil
1 cup semolina
½ cup sugar
1 teaspoon
   ground cardamom
3 cups water
½ cup chopped
   mixed nuts (such as
   cashews, almonds,
   and pistachios)

1. Select Sauté mode, adjust the heat to high, and put the oil in the Instant Pot.

2. Once the oil starts to warm up, add the semolina and cook for 3 to 4 minutes, stirring occasionally to keep it from burning.

3. Slowly stir in the sugar and cardamom and mix well.

4. Add the water and stir well to combine.

5. Turn off Sauté mode, lock the lid, and close the steam valve. Press Manual and set the timer for 2 minutes on high pressure.

6. When the timer goes off, let the pressure release naturally for about 10 minutes, then quick release any remaining pressure. Carefully remove the lid.

7. Top with the mixed nuts and serve warm.

PREP TIP: The semolina should turn a pale golden color once it has been toasted properly. Be careful not to let it burn by stirring occasionally to prevent it from sticking to the bottom of the pot.

VARIATION: A popular variation of this recipe in many Indian homes involves substituting semolina with Indian whole-wheat flour, also known as atta.

Per serving: Calories: 305; Total fat: 14g; Saturated fat: 2g; Sodium: 2mg; Carbohydrates: 40g; Sugar: 17g; Fiber: 2g; Protein: 6g; Calcium: 10mg

MOONG DAL HALWA (YELLOW MOONG HALWA)

GLUTEN-FREE, SOY-FREE

Prep time: 5 minutes **Sauté time:** 5 minutes **Pressure build:** 8 to 10 minutes **Pressure cook:** 5 minutes **Pressure release:** Natural, 10 minutes **Total time:** 35 minutes **Serves 6**

In this version of halwa, yellow moong lentils are used. Yellow moong lentils are the split version of green moong lentils. (See page 6 for details.) Halwa is slightly denser than kheer and has a creamy texture very similar to oatmeal or porridge.

¼ cup neutral cooking oil
1 cup yellow moong lentils, rinsed
½ cup sugar
1 teaspoon ground cardamom
3 cups water
½ cup chopped mixed nuts (such as cashews, almonds, and pistachios)

1. Select Sauté mode, adjust the heat to high, and put the oil in the Instant Pot.

2. Once the oil starts to warm up, add the lentils and cook for 5 minutes, stirring occasionally to avoid burning.

3. Slowly stir in the sugar and cardamom and mix well. Add the water and stir well to combine.

4. Turn off Sauté mode, lock the lid, and close the steam valve. Press Manual and set the timer for 5 minutes on high pressure.

5. When the timer goes off, let the pressure release naturally for about 10 minutes, then quick release any remaining pressure. Carefully remove the lid.

6. Top with the mixed nuts and serve warm.

PREP TIP: The moong lentils should turn a darker golden hue once they have been toasted properly. Stir regularly to prevent the lentils from burning and sticking to the bottom of the pot.

Per serving: Calories: 325; Total fat: 14g; Saturated fat: 2g; Sodium: 12mg; Carbohydrates: 41g; Sugar: 18g; Fiber: 4g; Protein: 11g; Calcium: 19mg

MANGO KHEER (MANGO RICE PUDDING)

GLUTEN-FREE, SOY-FREE

Prep time: 5 minutes **Pressure build:** 14 minutes total **Pressure cook:** 5 minutes, then 2 minutes **Pressure release:** Quick, then Natural, 10 minutes **Total time:** 36 minutes **Serves 6**

Mango kheer is a colorful, sweet, and slightly tangy rice pudding made with coconut milk and flavored with mango. Although using fresh mango will always give you the best result, you can opt for thawed frozen mango if you need to.

4 cups water

1 cup basmati rice, rinsed

1½ cups full-fat coconut milk

½ cup sugar

1 teaspoon ground cardamom

2 cups finely chopped fresh mango (or frozen and thawed)

1. Put the water and rice in the Instant Pot. Lock the lid, close the steam valve, and set the timer for 5 minutes on high pressure.

2. When the timer goes off, quick release the pressure.

3. Open the lid carefully and slowly stir in the coconut milk, sugar, and cardamom to mix well.

4. Lock the lid, close the steam valve, and set the timer for 2 minutes on high pressure. When the timer goes off, let the pressure release naturally for about 10 minutes, then quick release any remaining pressure. Carefully remove the lid.

5. Top with the mango right before serving.

VARIATION: Serve this either warm or cold depending on your preference. You can jazz it up by topping it with some chopped nuts and/or toasted coconut flakes.

Per serving: Calories: 307; Total fat: 11g; Saturated fat: 9g; Sodium: 7mg; Carbohydrates: 52g; Sugar: 26g; Fiber: 1g; Protein: 3g; Calcium: 10mg

SAFFRON KHEER (SAFFRON RICE PUDDING)

GLUTEN-FREE, SOY-FREE

Prep time: 5 minutes **Pressure build:** 14 minutes total **Pressure cook:** 5 minutes, then 2 minutes **Pressure release:** Quick, then Natural, 10 minutes **Total time:** 36 minutes **Serves 6**

This rice pudding is made with coconut milk and flavored with saffron. Kheer is usually served on special occasions like festivals or weddings.

4 cups water
1 cup basmati rice, rinsed
1½ cups full-fat coconut milk
½ cup sugar
1 teaspoon ground cardamom
¼ teaspoon saffron
½ cup chopped pistachios

1. Put the water and rice in the Instant Pot. Lock the lid, close the steam valve, and set the timer for 5 minutes on high pressure.

2. When the timer goes off, quick release the pressure.

3. Open the lid carefully and slowly stir in the coconut milk, sugar, cardamom, and saffron. Mix well.

4. Lock the lid, close the steam valve, and set the timer for 2 minutes on high pressure. When the timer goes off, let the pressure release naturally for about 10 minutes, then quick release any remaining pressure. Carefully remove the lid.

5. Top with the pistachios right before serving.

VARIATION: This recipe can be served warm or cold depending on your preference. You can also add in chopped cashews instead of pistachios.

Per serving: Calories: 331; Total fat: 16g; Saturated fat: 10g; Sodium: 6mg; Carbohydrates: 47g; Sugar: 20g; Fiber: 2g; Protein: 5g; Calcium: 14mg

GAJAR HALWA (CARROT HALWA)

GLUTEN-FREE, SOY-FREE

Prep time: 10 minutes **Sauté time:** 5 minutes **Pressure build:** 8 to 10 minutes
Pressure cook: 2 minutes **Pressure release:** Natural, 10 minutes
Total time: 37 minutes **Serves 6**

This traditional Indian homestyle pudding is made using freshly grated carrots. Since carrots are abundant in the winter season in India, this recipe tends to be enjoyed during the cold winter months.

¼ cup neutral cooking oil
4 cups grated carrots
½ cup sugar
1 teaspoon ground cardamom
½ cup finely ground almonds
¼ cup thinly sliced almonds

1. Select Sauté mode, adjust the heat to high, and put the oil in the Instant Pot.

2. Once the oil starts to warm up, add the carrots and cook for about 5 minutes, stirring occasionally, until the moisture starts to evaporate.

3. Slowly stir in the sugar and cardamom and mix well.

4. Add the ground almonds and stir well to combine.

5. Turn off Sauté mode, lock the lid, and close the steam valve. Press Manual and set the timer for 2 minutes on high pressure.

6. When the timer goes off, let the pressure release naturally for about 10 minutes, then quick release any remaining pressure. Carefully remove the lid.

7. Top with the sliced almonds and serve warm.

INGREDIENT TIP: This recipe is best served warm with a dollop of vegan vanilla ice cream on the side. You can also add in chopped cashews instead of almonds.

Per serving: Calories: 251; Total fat: 16g; Saturated fat: 2g; Sodium: 51mg; Carbohydrates: 27g; Sugar: 21g; Fiber: 4g; Protein: 4g; Calcium: 60mg

GREEN MOONG KHEER (GREEN MOONG PUDDING)

GLUTEN-FREE, SOY-FREE

Prep time: 5 minutes **Pressure build:** 8 to 10 minutes **Pressure cook:** 10 minutes, then 2 minutes **Pressure release:** Quick, then Natural, 10 minutes **Total time:** 37 minutes **Serves 6**

This is a grain-free version of the classic kheer made from coconut milk and green moong lentils. If you've never enjoyed lentils as a dessert, you're in for a treat. Keep in mind that it will thicken up as it cools.

3 cups water
1 cup dried green moong lentils, rinsed
1½ cups full-fat coconut milk
½ cup sugar
¼ teaspoon salt

1. Put the water and lentils in the Instant Pot. Lock the lid, close the steam valve, and set the timer for 10 minutes on high pressure.

2. When the timer goes off, quick release the pressure.

3. Open the lid carefully and slowly stir in the coconut milk, sugar, and salt. Mix well.

4. Lock the lid, close the steam valve, and set the timer for 2 minutes on high pressure.

5. When the timer goes off, let the pressure release naturally for about 10 minutes, then quick release any remaining pressure. Carefully remove the lid. Serve.

VARIATION: This recipe can either be served warm or cold depending on your preference.

Per serving: Calories: 286; Total fat: 11g; Saturated fat: 9g; Sodium: 111mg; Carbohydrates: 41g; Sugar: 21g; Fiber: 6g; Protein: 9g; Calcium: 49mg

BESAN BARFI (INDIAN-STYLE FUDGE)

GLUTEN-FREE, SOY-FREE

Prep time: 5 minutes **Sauté time:** 5 minutes **Pressure build:** 8 to 10 minutes
Pressure cook: 4 minutes **Pressure release:** Natural, 10 minutes
Total time: 34 minutes **Serves 6**

This is a traditional Indian-style fudge made from chickpea flour, sugar, and cardamom, and is garnished with chopped mixed nuts. Feel free to experiment with the garnish, using other nuts, coconut flakes, or even rose petals for a colorful presentation.

¼ cup neutral cooking oil
1 cup chickpea flour
   (besan)
½ cup sugar
1 teaspoon ground
   cardamom
3 cups water
½ cup chopped
   mixed nuts (such as
   cashews, almonds,
   and pistachios)

1. Select Sauté mode, adjust the heat to high, and put the oil in the Instant Pot.

2. Once the oil the starts to warm up, add the flour and cook for 3 to 4 minutes, stirring occasionally to avoid burning.

3. Slowly stir in the sugar and cardamom and mix well. Add the water and stir well to combine.

4. Turn off Sauté mode, lock the lid, and close the steam valve. Press Manual and set the timer for 4 minutes on high pressure.

5. When the timer goes off, let the pressure release naturally for about 10 minutes.

6. Stir in the mixed nuts and spoon out the fudge onto a greased baking sheet. Spread it with a spatula, roughly ½-inch thick.

7. Cut into squares, let it cool, and serve at room temperature.

PREP TIP: The besan, or chickpea flour, should turn a darker golden hue once it has been toasted properly. Be careful not to let it burn by stirring occasionally to prevent it from sticking to the bottom of the pot.

Per serving: Calories: 285; Total fat: 15g; Saturated fat: 2g; Sodium: 2mg; Carbohydrates: 34g; Sugar: 18g; Fiber: 4g; Protein: 5g; Calcium: 27mg

COCONUT LADOOS (COCONUT FUDGE)

GLUTEN-FREE, SOY-FREE, SUPER FAST

Prep time: 5 minutes **Pressure build:** 8 to 10 minutes **Pressure cook:** 1 minute
Pressure release: Natural, 10 minutes **Total time:** 26 minutes **Serves 6**

These Indian-style fudge balls are made with coconut and chopped nuts. They come together quickly and are a tasty treat to share with friends or family—or to enjoy all on your own! I use almonds here but feel free to mix and match with other nuts, if desired.

3 cups dried
   coconut flakes
½ cup sugar
½ cup full-fat
   coconut milk
1 tablespoon coconut oil
1 cup finely chopped
   almonds

1. Put the coconut flakes, sugar, coconut milk, and coconut oil in the Instant Pot and stir to combine. Lock the lid, close the steam valve, and set the timer for 1 minute on high pressure.

2. When the timer goes off, let the pressure release naturally for about 10 minutes, then quick release any remaining pressure.

3. Open the lid carefully and slowly stir in the almonds to mix well.

4. Let the mixture cool completely; then, using a mini ice-cream scoop, spoon out balls of the fudge and serve.

PREP TIP: Depending on the brand of coconut milk you use, you might find the fudge to be slightly runny. If so, you can simply roll the balls in desiccated coconut or coconut flakes to get a clean, firm texture.

Per serving: Calories: 508; Total fat: 42g; Saturated fat: 29g; Sodium: 17mg; Carbohydrates: 32g; Sugar: 21g; Fiber: 9g; Protein: 8g; Calcium: 70mg

KHAJUR KI MITHAI (DATE SQUARES)

GLUTEN-FREE, SOY-FREE, SUPER FAST

Prep time: 5 minutes **Pressure build:** 8 to 10 minutes **Pressure cook:** 2 minutes
Pressure release: Quick **Total time:** 17 minutes **Serves 6**

These Indian-style date squares are made with Medjool dates and chopped nuts, and are almost like a fudge. They're fairly quick and easy to put together and are a perfect sweet treat or snack. You can change up the nuts to your liking and try it out with different variations.

2 cups Medjool
    dates, pitted and
    roughly chopped
½ cup water
1 tablespoon coconut oil
¼ teaspoon ground
    cardamom
¼ cup chopped almonds
¼ cup chopped cashews
¼ cup chopped pistachios

1. Put the dates, water, coconut oil, and cardamom in the Instant Pot and stir to mix well. Lock the lid, close the steam valve, and set the timer for 2 minutes on high pressure.

2. When the timer goes off, quick release the pressure.

3. Open the lid carefully and slowly stir in the nuts to mix well.

4. Spread out the mixture evenly, making sure to smooth the top surface.

5. Let the mixture cool completely; then cut into bite-size squares and serve.

Per serving: Calories: 332; Total fat: 10g; Saturated fat: 3g; Sodium: 2mg; Carbohydrates: 64g; Sugar: 54g; Fiber: 7g; Protein: 5g; Calcium: 74mg

BEETROOT RAITA, page 106

CHAPTER SEVEN

BASICS

MANGO CHUTNEY

GLUTEN-FREE, NUT-FREE, SOY-FREE, SUPER FAST

Prep time: 10 minutes **Makes about 1 cup**

This is a sweet and tangy chutney made with fresh mangoes and mint. This chutney is great with fried snacks like samosas and even pairs extremely well with wraps or sandwiches. Fresh mango works best, but frozen, thawed mango can be used in its place to save on prep time.

1 large ripe mango, peeled and chopped
8 to 10 fresh mint leaves
2 tablespoons freshly squeezed lemon juice
1 tablespoon sugar
Salt

In a food processor, blend the mango, mint, lemon juice, and sugar and season with salt. Blend until smooth. Serve cold.

INGREDIENT TIP: This chutney should have a balanced sweet and tart flavor. If your mango lacks in sweetness, increase the amount of sugar a bit.

VARIATION: You can alter this recipe by using fresh pineapple or peaches instead of mangoes. Both variations work well with Indian flavors and make a great addition to any meal.

Per ¼-cup serving: Calories: 64; Total fat: <1g; Saturated fat: <1g; Sodium: 1mg; Carbohydrates: 16g; Sugar: 15g; Fiber: 1g; Protein: 1g; Calcium: 10mg

TOMATO CHUTNEY

GLUTEN-FREE, NUT-FREE, SOY-FREE, SUPER FAST

Prep time: 10 minutes **Sauté time:** 5 minutes **Total time:** 15 minutes **Makes about 2 cups**

This warm tomato-based chutney pairs well with Keema Pulao (page 83), Palak Rice (page 53), and Tehri (page 55). Though made to complement curries, it's also tasty as a sandwich spread or as a dipping sauce.

1 tablespoon neutral cooking oil
1 teaspoon mustard seeds
1 teaspoon cumin seeds
1 tablespoon minced garlic
3 or 4 fresh curry leaves
2 large tomatoes, finely chopped
½ teaspoon ground red chili
¼ teaspoon ground turmeric
Salt

1. Select Sauté mode, adjust the heat to low, and put the oil, mustard seeds, and cumin seeds in the Instant Pot.

2. Once the mustard and cumin seeds start to sizzle, add the garlic and curry leaves and fry for a few seconds until fragrant. Keep stirring occasionally to avoid burning.

3. Add the tomatoes, red chili, and turmeric and cook for about 5 minutes, until the tomatoes start to pulp and blend in with the spices.

4. Season with salt and serve warm.

PREP TIP: When making a big batch, store this tomato chutney in clean tightly sealing glass jars in the refrigerator, and it will stay fresh for about 1 week. You can also freeze a batch for up to 3 months.

INGREDIENT TIP: The tomatoes need to cook down to pulp to get a thick consistency for this chutney. You can add a bit of water if the tomatoes are too firm to pulp on their own.

Per ¼-cup serving: Calories: 29; Total fat: 2g; Saturated fat: <1g; Sodium: 3mg; Carbohydrates: 2g; Sugar: 1g; Fiber: 1g; Protein: 1g; Calcium: 15mg

MINT CHUTNEY

GLUTEN-FREE, NUT-FREE, SOY-FREE, SUPER FAST

Prep time: 10 minutes **Makes 2 cups**

This is a classic raw green chutney served with many of the popular Indian snacks, such as samosas and pakoras. It's also delicious with Vegetable Biryani (page 46) and Chana Pulao (page 50). It's made with a mix of green chiles, fresh cilantro, and mint.

1 cup chopped fresh
    mint leaves
1 cup chopped fresh
    cilantro leaves
2 tablespoons freshly
    squeezed lemon juice
1 green chile (shishito,
    jalapeño, or
    banana pepper),
    roughly chopped
1 or 2 tablespoons water
1 garlic clove, peeled
¼ teaspoon ground cumin
Salt

In a blender, blend the mint, cilantro, lemon juice, chile, water, garlic, and cumin. Season with salt and process until smooth. Serve cold.

INGREDIENT TIP: When picking mint and cilantro, always remember to select a bunch that is as fresh as possible with vibrant green leaves.

Per ¼-cup serving: Calories: 5; Total fat: <1g; Saturated fat: <1g; Sodium: 2mg; Carbohydrates: 1g; Sugar: <1g; Fiber: <1g; Protein: <1g; Calcium: 11mg

INSTANT CHILE ACHAAR (QUICK GREEN CHILE PICKLES)

GLUTEN-FREE, NUT-FREE, SOY-FREE, SUPER FAST

Prep time: 5 minutes **Sauté time:** 10 minutes **Total time:** 15 minutes **Makes about 2 cups**

A quick homestyle version of classic green chile pickles, these are served with meals at many Indian restaurants. A little goes a long way to add a burst of flavor and heat to dishes. If you want less heat, remove the seeds or choose milder chiles. Serve it alongside Dal Tadka (page 21) or Dal Makhani (page 76).

1 tablespoon neutral cooking oil

1 teaspoon Paanch Phoron (page 112)

12 to 15 fresh large green chiles (shishito, jalapeño, or banana peppers), cut into ½-inch pieces

1 teaspoon amchur powder

1 teaspoon sugar

Salt

1. Select Sauté mode, adjust the heat to high, and put the oil and paanch phoron in the Instant Pot.

2. Once the paanch phoron starts to sizzle, add the chiles and stir-fry for 5 to 6 minutes, until they begin to blister and soften.

3. Mix in the amchur powder and sugar and season with salt. Stir-fry for another 1 to 2 minutes, until everything is mixed well.

4. Serve as an accompaniment with rice and dal.

INGREDIENT TIP: When picking green chiles, always remember that the larger it is, the less spicy it will be. For a milder version of this pickle, jalapeños or banana peppers work really well.

Per ¼-cup serving: Calories: 42; Total fat: 2g; Saturated fat: <1g; Sodium: 2mg; Carbohydrates: 6g; Sugar: 3g; Fiber: 2g; Protein: 1g; Calcium: 10mg

BEETROOT RAITA

GLUTEN-FREE, NUT-FREE, SOY-FREE, SUPER FAST

Prep time: 10 minutes **Makes about 1 cup**

This is another version of a simple raita made with grated beetroot. It's colorful, cooling, and great with spicy dishes. Try it alongside Vegetable Biryani (page 46) or Keema Pulao (page 83).

1 cup plain vegan yogurt, beaten until smooth (confirm nut-free if needed)
¾ cup grated beetroot
1 tablespoon minced fresh cilantro leaves
¼ teaspoon ground cumin
¼ teaspoon ground red chili
Salt

In a medium bowl, mix the yogurt, beetroot, cilantro, cumin, and red chili. Season with salt and serve cold.

PREP TIP: Raita is best enjoyed as soon as it is prepared. If you let it sit for too long, it starts to extract more moisture and lose its flavor—especially when fresh herbs are added.

Per ¼-cup serving: Calories: 65; Total fat: 5g; Saturated fat: <1g; Sodium: 46mg; Carbohydrates: 7g; Sugar: 4g; Fiber: 2g; Protein: 2g; Calcium: 25mg

CUCUMBER RAITA

GLUTEN-FREE, NUT-FREE, SOY-FREE, SUPER FAST

Prep time: 10 minutes **Makes about 1 cup**

The classic pairing to any Indian meal, cucumber raita is a yogurt dip made with fresh grated cucumber and seasoned lightly with spices. Serve it as a side with any dish consisting of rice and lentils.

1 cup plain vegan yogurt, beaten until smooth (confirm nut-free if needed)
¾ cup grated cucumber
1 tablespoon minced fresh mint leaves
¼ teaspoon ground cumin
¼ teaspoon ground red chili
Salt

In a medium bowl, mix the yogurt, cucumber, mint, cumin, and red chili. Season with salt and serve cold.

INGREDIENT TIP: The grated cucumber will continue to release its own moisture the longer it sits. To avoid the raita thinning down too much, prepare this right before you're ready to serve.

Per ¼-cup serving: Calories: 47; Total fat: 5g; Saturated fat: <1g; Sodium: 5mg; Carbohydrates: 3g; Sugar: 1g; Fiber: 1g; Protein: 2g; Calcium: 22mg

TOMATO RAITA

GLUTEN-FREE, NUT-FREE, SOY-FREE, SUPER FAST

Prep time: 10 minutes **Makes about 1 cup**

In this version of raita, fresh tomatoes come together with a few fresh herbs and spices to jazz up plain yogurt. The tomatoes add a subtle sweetness to the plain yogurt and give it some texture.

1 cup plain vegan yogurt, beaten until smooth (confirm nut-free if needed)

1 cup finely chopped tomatoes

1 tablespoon fresh cilantro leaves, minced

1 tablespoon fresh mint leaves, minced

¼ teaspoon cumin powder

¼ teaspoon red chili powder

Salt

In a medium bowl, mix the yogurt, tomatoes, cilantro, mint, cumin, and chili powder. Season with salt and serve cold.

Per ¼-cup serving: Calories: 51; Total fat: 3g; Saturated fat: 1g; Sodium: 9mg; Carbohydrates: 5g; Sugar: 2g; Fiber: 1g; Protein: 2g; Calcium: 16mg

KACHUMBER (INDIAN-STYLE CHOPPED SALAD)

GLUTEN-FREE, NUT-FREE, SOY-FREE, SUPER FAST

Prep time: 10 minutes **Makes 2 cups**

This Indian-style salad is most commonly made with finely chopped onions, tomatoes, and cucumbers, with a splash of fresh lemon juice. If you don't have chaat masala, you can also use an additional squeeze of fresh lemon juice.

1 cup finely chopped
   cucumber
1 cup finely chopped
   tomatoes
½ cup finely
   chopped onions
¼ cup finely chopped
   fresh cilantro leaves
¼ cup freshly squeezed
   lemon juice
¼ teaspoon chaat masala
Salt
Freshly ground
   black pepper

In a medium bowl, mix the cucumber, tomatoes, onions, cilantro, lemon juice, and chaat masala. Season with salt and pepper and serve cold.

Per 1-cup serving: Calories: 55; Total fat: <1g; Saturated fat: <1g; Sodium: 20mg; Carbohydrates: 13g; Sugar: 6g; Fiber: 3g; Protein: 2g; Calcium: 36mg

GARAM MASALA

GLUTEN-FREE, NUT-FREE, SOY-FREE, SUPER FAST

Prep time: 10 minutes **Sauté time:** 2 minutes **Makes about ¼ cup**

Garam masala is a warming spice blend made from a mix of various whole spices, typically used as a finishing spice in most curries. Almost every Indian home has its own secret recipe, varying by region and the amount of the spices used.

2 tablespoons
   coriander seeds
1 teaspoon cumin seeds
1 (1-inch) cinnamon stick
2 bay leaves
4 or 5 whole cloves
4 or 5 whole green
   cardamom pods

1. Select Sauté mode, adjust the heat to high, and put the coriander seeds, cumin seeds, cinnamon stick, bay leaves, cloves, and cardamom pods in the Instant Pot. Dry roast all the spices together for a couple of minutes until they start to get fragrant, being careful not to let them burn.

2. Let the spices cool a bit, then grind them to a fine powder in a spice grinder.

PREP TIP: This spice blend should be stored in a cool, dry place and keeps well for up to 1 month.

Per 1-tablespoon serving: Calories: 14; Total fat: 1g; Saturated fat: 0g; Sodium: 2mg; Carbohydrates: 3g; Sugar: 0g; Fiber: 2g; Protein: 1g; Calcium: 34mg

TANDOORI MASALA

GLUTEN-FREE, NUT-FREE, SOY-FREE, SUPER FAST

Prep time: 5 minutes **Makes 5 tablespoons**

This is a spice blend used in most grilled Indian recipes, mainly consisting of red chili, coriander, and garam masala. Try it with Achari Paneer Tikka (page 80) and Achari Gobi (page 62).

3 tablespoons ground
  coriander
1 tablespoon
  amchur powder
1 teaspoon ground
  red chili
1 teaspoon Garam Masala
  (page 110)
1 teaspoon chaat masala

In a small bowl, mix the coriander, amchur powder, red chili, garam masala, and chaat masala until well combined. Store it in a clean, dry jar with a tight lid.

PREP TIP: This spice blend should be stored in a cool, dry place and keeps well for up to 1 month.

Per 1-tablespoon serving: Calories: 26; Total fat: <1g; Saturated fat: 0g; Sodium: 20mg; Carbohydrates: 6g; Sugar: <1g; Fiber: <1g; Protein: <1g; Calcium: 17mg

PAANCH PHORON

GLUTEN-FREE, NUT-FREE, SOY-FREE, SUPER FAST

Prep time: 5 minutes **Makes 5 tablespoons**

A traditional spice mix from the region of Bengal, paanch phoron is typically used at the start of the cooking process as a tempering agent. It's made with five different spice seeds. If you can't find nigella seeds, also known as kalonji, you can substitute them with celery seeds.

1 tablespoon cumin seeds
1 tablespoon fennel seeds
1 tablespoon nigella seeds
1 tablespoon
   mustard seeds
1 tablespoon
   fenugreek seeds

In a small bowl, mix the cumin seeds, fennel seeds, nigella seeds, mustard seeds, and fenugreek seeds. Store in a clean, dry jar with a tight-fitting resealable lid.

INGREDIENT TIP: This spice blend should be stored in a cool, dry place and keeps well for up to 1 month.

Per 1-tablespoon serving: Calories: 37; Total fat: 2g; Saturated fat: <1g; Sodium: 5mg; Carbohydrates: 4g; Sugar: <1g; Fiber: 2g; Protein: 2g; Calcium: 32mg

MEASUREMENT CONVERSIONS

VOLUME EQUIVALENTS (LIQUID)

US STANDARD	US STANDARD (OUNCES)	METRIC (APPROX.)
2 tablespoons	1 fl. oz.	30 mL
¼ cup	2 fl. oz.	60 mL
½ cup	4 fl. oz.	120 mL
1 cup	8 fl. oz.	240 mL
1½ cups	12 fl. oz.	355 mL
2 cups or 1 pint	16 fl. oz.	475 mL
4 cups or 1 quart	32 fl. oz.	1 L
1 gallon	128 fl. oz.	4 L

OVEN TEMPERATURES

FAHRENHEIT (F)	CELSIUS (C) (APPROX.)
250°	120°
300°	150°
325°	165°
350°	180°
375°	190°
400°	200°
425°	220°
450°	230°

VOLUME EQUIVALENTS (DRY)

US STANDARD	METRIC (APPROX.)
⅛ teaspoon	0.5 mL
¼ teaspoon	1 mL
½ teaspoon	2 mL
¾ teaspoon	4 mL
1 teaspoon	5 mL
1 tablespoon	15 mL
¼ cup	59 mL
⅓ cup	79 mL
½ cup	118 mL
⅔ cup	156 mL
¾ cup	177 mL
1 cup	235 mL
2 cups or 1 pint	475 mL
3 cups	700 mL
4 cups or 1 quart	1 L

WEIGHT EQUIVALENTS

US STANDARD	METRIC (APPROX.)
½ ounce	15 g
1 ounce	30 g
2 ounces	60 g
4 ounces	115 g
8 ounces	225 g
12 ounces	340 g
16 ounces or 1 pound	455 g

RESOURCES

COOKBOOKS

- Agarwal, Meena. *500 Indian Dishes*. Apple Press, 2013.

- Agarwal, Meena. *Knack Indian Cooking: A Step-by-Step Guide to Authentic Dishes Made Easy*. Globe Pequot Press, 2010.

SPICES

If you can't find certain spices at your local supermarket or Indian grocer, try these online sources:

- Arvindas.com

- DiasporaCo.com

- SpiceWallaBrand.com

- TheSpicyGourmet.com

INDEX

ACKNOWLEDGMENTS

My editor Anna Pulley and the entire Callisto team, you are all rock stars, and this book wouldn't have come to life without you. My family and friends, you always come ready with a spoon to taste anything out of my kitchen, and with a smile on your face! And most importantly, my blog readers, after all these years you still inspire me to keep cooking.

I thank you all for your love and support. Happy eating!

ABOUT THE AUTHOR

Meena Agarwal is a Toronto-based food writer, cooking instructor, and recipe developer. She is the creator of the award-winning food blog *Hooked on Heat* (HookedOnHeat.com) and author of two previously published cookbooks, *Knack Indian Cooking* and *500 Indian Dishes*.

Meena's writing and food reflect the eclectic tastes she has gathered from her Indian and Malaysian heritage, as well as her travels around the globe.

CPSIA information can be obtained
at www.ICGtesting.com
Printed in the USA
BVHW020928160921
616887BV00017B/568